THE WORLD ACCORDING TO

MARGARET THATCHER

THE WORLD
ACCORDING TO
MARGARET
THATCHER

STEPHEN BLAKE
AND
ANDREW JOHN

MICHAEL O'MARA BOOKS LIMITED

First published in Great Britain in 2003 by
Michael O'Mara Books Limited
9 Lion Yard
Tremadoc Road
London SW4 7NQ

A CIP catalogue record for this book is available from
the British Library

ISBN 1-84317-015-9

1 3 5 7 9 10 8 6 4 2

Designed and typeset by Design 23

Printed and bound in Finland by WS Bookwell, Juva

CONTENTS

PREFACE

Anyone who watched television news that night in November 1990 will recall the image of a tearful Margaret Thatcher in the back of a car, being driven away from Number 10 Downing Street. It was poignant and dramatic, coming as it did at the end of a bitter leadership battle. Those same pictures saturated acres of newsprint the following day. She was saying goodbye to what had been her official home for eleven and a half years.

Mention the name 'Thatcher' and you stir emotion. That emotion manifests itself across a broad spectrum, but most of it is concentrated at one end or the other: you love her or you hate her. What cannot be denied is that, this passionate politician, pursuing single-mindedly her ideal of individualism, and fighting collectivism wherever she might find it, was a phenomenon.

Margaret Thatcher was the daughter of a grocer and went on to become not only Britain's first woman prime minister, but the first in European history. For a woman to achieve that degree of political clout even in the first decade of the twenty-first century is hard to imagine. She did it in 1979, and in a party that knew nothing of such ideas as all-women candidate lists and positive discrimination.

However, she had a high opinion of women, and once said that they were an immensely practical sex. They got on with the job, and didn't talk about it as much as men.

During her premiership, a distinctive monetary policy

was adopted, and government interference was reduced. There was also a determination to curb public spending, leading to friction between local and central government.

By the time she resigned in November 1990, one in four of the population owned shares and more than forty former state-owned businesses had been privatized. The BT sell-off of 1984 was followed by the privatization of British Gas in 1986 and of Rolls-Royce, British Airways and the British Airports Authority in 1987.

Of course, many who had worked in the old nationalized industries subsequently lost their jobs, as the important bottom line depended on leanness for its own health, and the fat cats of the newly privatized companies sought constantly to trim outgoings and maximize income for avaricious shareholders.

Mrs Thatcher's government was also the one that fought for sovereignty in the South Atlantic, survived a bomb explosion in a Brighton hotel, did battle with King Coal himself, Arthur Scargill, during the 1984–5 miners' strike, gave us the hated poll tax and introduced the equally detested Section 28. While the others are consigned to the history books, important though they are, only the last of these remains a campaigning issue to this day.

Even in her seventies and after a number of minor strokes, Baroness Thatcher has a good deal of stamina, and famously needed only about four hours' sleep a night during her time as Prime Minister. And, while battling for the Tories before the 1991 general election, she dubbed her campaign 'the Mummy returns'.

This is a short biography of one of the most outstanding politicians of the twentieth century – and whether you interpret the word 'outstanding' as being for good or bad will depend on your political persuasions.

Either way, there is no doubt that her achievements are remarkable for a woman from a poor background, and her story is a fascinating one.

If your appetite for information about the life of Margaret Hilda Thatcher has been whetted, you will benefit from our suggestions for further reading at the back of this book.

STEPHEN BLAKE AND ANDREW JOHN
FEBRUARY 2003

LIFE BEFORE LEADERSHIP:
Margaret's Road to Power

I had very little "privilege" in my early years.
1975

In 1925 John Logie Baird transmitted the first television broadcast from his laboratory; Al Capone took over the bootlegging racket in Chicago; Ben-Hur, costing a record-breaking $3.95 million to make, was released; the worst tornado in American history hit Illinois and Indiana. And, on 13 October, Margaret Hilda Roberts was born in Grantham, Lincolnshire, second daughter of Alfred and Beatrice Roberts.

Margaret's father was a grocer who owned a corner shop on the Great North Road. Alfred had started out from a very poor background, and he brought his daughters up in the puritanical mould, with few luxuries and with the emphasis very much laid on hard work and parsimony. Most accounts of Margaret's early days leave one with the image of a home run strictly in accordance with Victorian values, and of familial duties performed without question and with a great sense of obligation:

‘I was brought up by a Victorian Grandmother. We were taught to … prove yourself. We were taught self-reliance. We were taught to live within our incomes.

We were taught that cleanliness is next to Godliness. We were taught self-respect. You were taught tremendous pride in your country. All of these things are Victorian values. They are perennial values.'

Margaret's mother, Beatrice Stephenson, was born at 10 South Parade in Grantham (it's now number 55). She could hardly have thought that her 'Number 10' was a precursor to *the* Number 10, which would be occupied by her daughter from 1979 to 1990.

Alfred and Beatie – as he called Beatrice – had saved enough money to marry by 1917, and two years later they had taken out a mortgage on the North Parade premises that were to be his famous grocer's shop, which was bought as a going concern.

Alfred was also to become a town councillor in Grantham, although his political affiliations were somewhat woolly: he has been described as a closet Conservative and a 'moderate' Labourite, as well as a Gladstonian Liberal. The way Margaret remembers it, you didn't fight local council elections as a party member back then. It just wasn't the done thing. Alfred stood as an independent – but, as his daughter acknowledged in later years, at heart he was a conservative:

'My father would in earlier years probably have been a Liberal Party voter, but that was when the Liberals stood for small government and private-enterprise economics. For as long as I remember our family was true-blue Tory.'

Alfred, just as his daughter would in 1979, achieved a political first: he became the town's youngest alderman in 1943. He also became the mayor of Grantham in 1945.

Alfred was a fundamentalist when it came to religion. His religion was entirely Bible-based – and this, along with the religious nature of his wife, was to have a considerable influence on the future Prime Minister of Great Britain and Northern Ireland. He did not approve of popular protest, being a great believer in upholding authority, as evidenced by his attitude towards the Jarrow marchers in 1936, when, as Margaret Thatcher was to say in 1975, 'He did not think that what they were doing was right.' In the matter of collectivism, as in others, Margaret was to turn out to be very much her father's daughter.

The Roberts family were Methodists, and Margaret was brought up with a very strong sense of duty: duty to one's spiritual side, and duty to provide for oneself and for one's family. Her upbringing contributed significantly to the development of her political philosophies, which emphasized the independence of the individual and the role of private charity, and which were opposed to socialism in all its many manifestations. Her family's brand of Methodism helped to instil the notion that what a person did voluntarily with his money was his own affair, and that giving in this way was morally superior to any welfare system financed by the taxpayer. This notion was expressed in its most extreme – and controversial – form in the autumn of 1987, when Margaret pronounced that there was 'no such thing as society':

'If children have a problem, it is [said to be] society that is at fault. There is no such thing as society. There is living tapestry of men and women and people and the beauty of that tapestry and the quality of our lives will depend upon how much each of us is prepared to take responsibility for ourselves.'

Though this proved to be a highly inflammatory comment, providing a great deal of ammunition for her opponents, it was a indication of her deep belief in the role of the individual, which would become such a defining feature of Thatcherism.

In later years Margaret Thatcher famously – or perhaps infamously – appeared to discount her mother's role when asked about her early family life. 'I owe almost everything to my father,' she once said. Even her *Who's Who* entry described her simply as the 'd. of Alfred Roberts, Grantham, Lincs', omitting all mention of Beatrice. In November 1985, she was quizzed by Dr Miriam Stoppard on a Yorkshire Television programme, *Woman to Woman*. She seemed to want to sidestep any discussion of her mother, wishing instead to concentrate on her father. 'Oh, Mummy backed up Daddy in everything,' she told her interviewer. Dr Stoppard persisted in her questioning, but, for all her efforts, extracted only grudging comments. For instance, when she asked Mrs Thatcher about familial discussions on current affairs, all she would say was, 'Mummy didn't get involved in the arguments. She had probably gone out to the kitchen to get the supper ready.'

However, years later, she did indirectly acknowledge that she owes something to her mother's housewifely skills. In her memoir, *The Path to Power*, she talks a little more about Beatrice, saying that she had learned from her 'what it meant to cope with a household so that everything worked like clockwork'. And, as she pointed out in 1979:

&Any woman who understands the problems of running a home will be nearer to understanding the problems of running a country.9

A first taste of politics

It could be argued that Margaret Thatcher's first taste of politics came when she helped at a local council election – although how significant an event she regarded it at the tender age of ten is difficult to say. She very much enjoyed it, though, as she revealed on BBC Radio Four's *Desert Island Discs* on 1 February 1978:

&I was only ten, but I do remember it, very vividly, and we used to go to the committee room and help. And the only way in which I could help was to run between the committee room and the polling station to get the lists of the numbers of people who'd voted and go and check them off. And I remember … it was quite a thrill for those of us working in the committee room when the candidate … came round and talked to us. And of course it never occurred to me that I'd be in the same position. *

The young Margaret Roberts attended Kesteven and Grantham Girls' School, where she was an exemplary, if reasonably quiet, pupil. She was one of the leading stars of the school's debating team, however – an early indication of the great public speaker she would turn out to be. Her first tentative foray into public life, albeit on a small scale, was made when she became head girl during her last term in the summer of 1943.

(This woman is headstrong, obstinate and dangerously self-opinionated.)
REPORT ON MARGARET ROBERTS BY THE ICI PERSONNEL DEPARTMENT

It was not long after her head-girlship that she finally found herself embroiled in politics proper. She undertook a degree course reading chemistry at Somerville College, Oxford, in October 1943 where, in addition to working hard at her degree, she became active in the Conservative Party. By June 1945 – at the age of nineteen – she was to be found addressing an election rally in Sleaford in Lincolnshire, in support of one Squadron Leader Worth and his Conservative candidacy. Nine months later, she addressed the conference of the Federation of

Conservative Students at the Waldorf Hotel in London, during which she seconded a motion calling for more working-class Conservative candidates. And, less than three years after that, in January 1949, Margaret herself was elected prospective parliamentary candidate to fight for the Labour-held seat of Dartford in Kent. A month later, when she was officially adopted as a candidate, she laid into the Labour government for its economic record.

> ❮ The charm of Britain has always been the ease with which one can move into the middle class. ❯
> 1974

Her career as a heavyweight speechmaker had begun. Speeches came thick and fast. Within weeks she was castigating Labour again, this time for their public-spending plans, when she spoke to the annual general meeting of Dartford Conservatives, before whose women's group the following month she called for a reduction in income tax.

Sloganeering was as creative then as it is now, and when Margaret Roberts was confirmed as the Conservative candidate, she went with the memorable slogan 'Vote right to keep what's left'. She was, however, unsuccessful in convincing the Labour-voting Dartford electorate that she was the right person for the job of being their Member of Parliament.

Was it that she was a woman? Was it that she was the youngest woman ever to contest the seat? Or was it merely that she was a Conservative? Perhaps the last of these was the main reason for her defeat, but certainly in those times the other two factors may well have played a consolidating part in her downfall. Whatever the reasons for her lack of success, she was readopted as candidate and in October 1951 she contested the seat once again – but again was unsuccessful.

At this time she was working as a research chemist at a plastics firm in Essex. As she later told Roy Plomley on *Desert Island Discs*:

⁶My first job was in a factory making plastics and it was in the development section. We were developing new plastics, taking them through the pilot stage and then thinking what they could be used for and where they could be sold. Sometimes I teased some of my Labour Members of Parliament friends and said, "You know, I've had more experience of working in a factory than you have."⁹

After that, she worked for the food firm Lyons in Hammersmith, London. However, neither of these two jobs consumed her in the way her interest in politics did, and in 1950 she began to read law. Though she had long had an interest in the subject, her decision was no doubt influenced by the consideration that at that time it seemed to be a far more suitable vocation for an aspiring politician.

It was while she was campaigning for the first time for

Dartford, that Margaret met her future husband, Denis. On *Desert Island Discs*, Roy Plomley asked her if she remembered the first night they first met:

> ❛I do, because it was the night that I was adopted as candidate and I had to get back to London, and I spoke to the meeting and it was thought that I obviously must circulate afterwards to get to know as many people as possible, and I missed the last train, so he was approached: would he like to drive me back to London? Mercifully, he did like, and so, eventually, did I.❜

In December 1951 the couple married, honeymooning in Portugal. Denis was to prove a great asset to Margaret's political career. As a man with a reasonable income, he was able to support her while she read for the Bar, and later, when they had children – Margaret gave birth to twins, Mark and Carol, in 1953 – he was able to pay for a nanny to enable Margaret to continue with her career. This was no doubt very helpful to her when it came to choosing to pursue a career in politics.

❛ It is expensive to be in politics. One has to be mobile, one has to be well groomed, and one has to entertain. ❜
1962

A safe seat at last

Mrs Thatcher's next attempt at a candidature was for Orpington in Kent in 1955, but she was rejected, and subsequently removed her name from the party's candidates list. (She was back on it in February 1956, however.)

A general election was held in 1955, and Mrs Thatcher spoke publicly in favour of the man she would eventually usurp as leader of the Conservative Party, Edward Heath.

Two years later, in January 1958, the voice that was to become one of the most loved and most reviled on British television and radio was heard for the first time when Margaret Thatcher gave a television interview to the BBC's *In Your Own Time*, in which she spoke about her short career as a barrister.

> We want a society in which we are free to make choices, to make mistakes, to be generous and compassionate. That is what we mean by a moral society – not a society in which the State is responsible for everything, and no one is responsible for the State.
> 1977

The law was soon behind her, however, and a bigger part in politics was about to begin, because, also in 1958, Margaret Hilda Thatcher, at the relatively young age of thirty-two, was selected as the prospective parliamentary candidate for the constituency she would eventually represent: the safe seat of Finchley. Later that year she was officially adopted as the Tory parliamentary candidate for the constituency, and in October 1959 she finally entered Westminster as the Honourable Member for Finchley.

Overwork and tragedy

The election that brought Margaret Thatcher to the House of Commons in 1959 was the Conservatives' third successive general election victory. The party now had a majority of one hundred. Not only were the party's fortunes on the rise, but the nation was also prospering, and Mrs Thatcher entered Westminster politics against the backdrop of exceptional growth rates among European and other Western countries.

> Look at a day when you are supremely satisfied at the end. It's not a day when you lounge around doing nothing; it's when you've had everything to do and you've done it.

It wasn't long before Mrs Thatcher was making herself known, both within the Palace of Westminster and outside it. Less than a month after her election, she came second in the ballot for private members' bills. On 8

January 1960 she appeared for the first time on Radio Four's *Any Questions*, and in February, her maiden speech in the Commons concerned her private members' bill, which was aimed at allowing the press to report local council meetings.

> ❝ After all, aren't I working class?
> I work jolly hard, I can tell you. ❞
> 1969

Famous for needing only four hours' sleep during her eleven years as premier, Mrs Thatcher's discipline and diligence was very much in evidence even then. For example, her maiden speech was extremely well researched, showed little reliance on her notes, and went on for nearly half an hour. And, just thirteen months after entering the House of Commons, she fainted in the chamber and attributed the event to overtiredness.

In December 1960 she suffered her first family tragedy while an MP, when her mother, Beatrice, died in Grantham. Beatrice's death provided an emptiness in Margaret's life, one that 'could never be filled'. For Mrs Thatcher, her mother 'had been a great rock of family stability'.

> ❝ ... it was from my mother that I inherited the
> ability to organize and combine so many
> duties of an active life. ❞

A second tragedy

Margaret Thatcher had been the Honourable Member for Finchley for just two years when, under Harold Macmillan's leadership, she took up her first ministerial post as Joint Parliamentary Secretary for Pensions and National Insurance. In October 1964 the Conservatives lost the next general election but she held on to her portfolio, becoming the Opposition spokesperson on pensions.

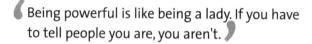

> Being powerful is like being a lady. If you have to tell people you are, you aren't.

In August 1965 Edward Heath became leader of the Conservative Party. Mrs Thatcher voted for him over Reginald Maudling and Enoch Powell, despite a close friendship with Maudling and a strong respect for Powell. Though she and Heath would later become the bitterest of enemies, at the time her loyalty did not go unrewarded for, in October of that same year, Heath gave her the portfolio of Housing and Land, and, by April 1966, she had been appointed to the shadow Treasury team under Iain McLeod.

In October 1967 Mrs Thatcher joined the Shadow Cabinet in charge of fuel and power. However, in November the following year, there was a Cabinet reshuffle, and Mrs Thatcher then became shadow transport spokesperson. Less than a year after that she was on the way to her first government job, when she was appointed shadow education spokesperson.

Meanwhile, however, Margaret suffered her second family tragedy while an MP, when her father, Alfred, died in Grantham. She went to visit him shortly before his death:

> ‘While I was there, friends from the church, business, local politics, the Rotary and bowling club, kept dropping in "just to see how Alf was". I hoped that at the end of my life I too would have so many good friends.’

Thatcher the milk snatcher

In 1970 the Conservative government was back in power, and Mrs Thatcher experienced her first taste of life as a cabinet minister, in charge of Education and Science. By this time, the swinging sixties – the decade that had seen love-ins and drugs, some relaxation of laws against gay sex and divorce – were over. Harold Wilson's 1964–70 government had sought to end the secondary school system that seemed to work in favour of brighter pupils, had prescribed equal pay for equal work for women, had abolished the death penalty and had lowered the age of majority from twenty-one to eighteen. Britain was a very different place from when the Tories had last been in power.

Those early days gave Mrs Thatcher the opportunity

to see from the lofty position of government the 'enemy' she would eventually trample: the trade unions. She saw at first hand just what a liability they could be for the government when, in 1971, Edward Heath tried to curb their power, leading to a series of damaging and brutal confrontations. The number of working days lost to industrial action in 1972 was greater than in any year since the General Strike of 1926.

Mrs Thatcher's first taste of public notoriety came in the autumn of 1971, when she came under attack for withdrawing the right to free milk for eight- to eleven-year-old primary-school children. The press gave her the nickname 'Thatcher the milk snatcher' and the *Sun* labelled her 'the most unpopular woman in Britain'. The experience, while bruising at the time, served to toughen her up considerably, and stood her in good stead for the even more turbulent times to come.

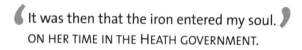

❨ It was then that the iron entered my soul. ❩
ON HER TIME IN THE HEATH GOVERNMENT.

Meanwhile, matters in the wider world were having a profound effect on Britain. There was an oil crisis, which only served to make the country's economic problems worse. Heath made the decision to float the pound – freeing Britain's currency from its earlier fixed rates set against other currencies. And, not for the first time, he sought admission to what was known then as the

Common Market (it was to become the European Economic Community, and subsequently the European Community, and eventually the EU, or the European Union).

The end of an era

Back in 1970, Edward Heath had ridden to power largely on the back of election promises to kick-start an economic recovery by tackling the powerful trade unions and instigating more free-market policies. In the event, his administration became noted for a series of U-turns as inflation forced the imposition of wage and price controls. Dire relationships between the government and the unions led to a series of miners' strikes, and by late 1973 these had so reduced energy supplies that a three-day week was introduced. In a bid to garner a mandate from the public in support of a strong stance against the miners, Heath held a general election in February 1974, but did not gain enough votes to form a Conservative government and was forced to resign as Prime Minister in March. Harold Wilson moved into Number 10, but, with only 301 seats to the Tories' 297, Labour had no overall majority. Another general election was held in October, when Labour won 319 seats and the Conservatives secured 277.

In the meantime, after the first general election defeat, Margaret Thatcher left the Department of Education and took up the post of shadow Environment Secretary. Along with Keith Joseph – who would later, under Mrs Thatcher's prime-ministership, become the education and science secretary – she founded the think tank known as the Centre for Policy Studies (CPS) in the spring of 1974, which was set up to study the comparative performances of European economies. In the event, it was to become something altogether more substantial. It held its first meeting at the House of Commons in June, before acquiring permanent premises in Wilfred Street, Westminster, in July. Keith Joseph was chairman and Mrs Thatcher jumped at the chance to become its vice-chairman. In *The Path to Power*, she describes the CPS as 'the powerhouse of alternative Conservative thinking on economic and social matters'. As she saw it, the CPS went on to develop 'the drive to expose the follies and self-defeating consequences of government intervention'.

❛ When I look at him and he looks at me, I don't feel that it is a man looking at a woman. More like a woman being looked at by another woman. ❜
ON EDWARD HEATH

In August 1974, she announced a pledge to abolish domestic rates and hold down mortgage interest rates to 9.5 per cent. (The abolition of domestic rates and the imposition of what came to be known popularly as the 'poll tax' would happen, of course, but not until much later.)

In November, after his second election defeat, Heath appointed Mrs Thatcher as Deputy Treasury spokesperson, under Robert Carr. November would also turn out to be even more significant for the future of Margaret Thatcher, and for the nation as a whole, for it was the month in which she decided to stand as leader of the Conservative Party.

LADY IN WAITING:

Margaret Becomes a Leader of Men

No woman in my time will be Prime Minister or Foreign Secretary – not the top jobs. Anyway I wouldn't want to be Prime Minister. You have to give yourself one hundred per cent to the job.
1969

After losing three out of four elections it was clear towards the end of 1974 that Edward Heath's days as leader of the Conservative Party were numbered. What was far from clear, however, was that Margaret Hilda Thatcher would end up being his successor.

Entering the leadership contest on 21 November, Mrs Thatcher was viewed initially as a stalking-horse candidate. Few anticipated the outcome of the second ballot in February 1975 when she won 146 votes, comfortably more than the 139 she needed to avoid a third. Enoch Powell is reputed to have said at the time, with not a little hint of envy in his voice, though making it sound like admiration:

She didn't rise to power. She was opposite the spot on the roulette wheel at the right time, and she didn't funk it.

Mrs Thatcher herself acknowledged that good fortune had its part to play:

You come to a certain time, and you look at the personalities available and their policies. And that's how women get on – right personality, right capability, right place at the right time.

At a news conference following her victory, she emphasized that all those who had been in Edward Heath's shadow Cabinet would remain – for the time being, anyway – in hers. 'I have asked the present people to stay in position for the time being,' she declared. 'I cannot act hastily. We shall try to make haste slowly.' The man she had usurped would be invited to join, too, but Edward Heath was not disposed to serve, and declined the offer to join the shadow Cabinet. He had, nevertheless, been among the first of Thatcher's rivals to wish her 'every success' in her leadership.

In Labour ranks, many viewed Mrs Thatcher's elevation to the honoured position of leader of the Conservative Party as a boon for the current Labour government. Though she must have felt somewhat awed by the prospect of being the first female leader of the Conservative Party, she kept any apprehensions she might have had well concealed. Asked how she felt about forthcoming clashes with the present PM, Harold Wilson, she replied, 'About the same as he feels facing me, I should think.'

In August that year, Mrs Thatcher made her first

foreign visit as the new Conservative leader when she went to Romania and met the notorious Nicolae Ceaucescu, who was the country's President from 1967 to 1989. He was noted for keeping his political opponents firmly in line, and, in the 1980s, would go on to impose a harsh austerity programme on his country in order to alleviate his country's foreign-debt problems. He imposed a cult of personality, while enforcing the relocation of large parts of the rural population. Ceaucescu was not a man for respecting human rights, and there were many demonstrations against his dictatorship. After the army had turned against him, he and his wife Elena tried to flee Bucharest, but he was captured and tried, and the Ceaucescus were executed on Christmas Day 1989.

After her Romania visit, Thatcher was soon globetrotting again, this time on a two-week visit to the United States and Canada.

Getting the unions in her sights

The next significant political event to hit the UK was the surprise resignation of Harold Wilson in March 1976. He announced that James Callaghan would become Britain's prime minister in his stead. More popular than his predecessor, Callaghan initially posed more of a challenge to the inexperienced Conservative leader in Commons debates. She conducted herself well, nevertheless, and soon made a name for herself, distinguishing herself as an excellent public speaker and political combatant. She had inherited a party loosely split between those still loyal to Heath, and those who wished to disassociate themselves from what they perceived to have been his leftist administration and move the party further towards the right. Though her own instincts led her to identify more closely with the latter group, in these early years, when her authority was far from unshakeable, she was careful to tread the middle ground with these factions. While appointing loyal Heathites such as James Prior and William Whitelaw to key positions in her shadow Cabinet she resisted elevating her key allies – men such as Keith Joseph, Geoffrey Howe and Norman Tebbit – who at this time were given relatively minor roles.

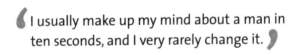

I usually make up my mind about a man in ten seconds, and I very rarely change it.

In March 1977 Margaret Thatcher was in combative mood after the Labour government had lost a vote on public expenditure. She moved a no-confidence vote. Six days later, the so-called Lib–Lab pact was formed between the Labour Party and David Steel's Liberals, in a move to sustain the government.

Mrs Thatcher did not bother to hide her distrust of the power of the trade unions when, in September of the same year, she was interviewed by Brian Walden on

Weekend World. He wanted to know how a Conservative government would deal with an all-out confrontation with the unions. While careful to add that she did not think that such a situation was likely to occur, she suggested that in such an event a future Tory government might hold a referendum. It was a statement that got her some good press, as well as backing from both wings of her party. She even set up a special party committee under the chairmanship of Nick Edwards, to report on the possible uses of a referendum. However, although the suggestion had bought some vital time for the Conservatives, it wasn't, she thought, the definitive answer to the problem, as she perceived it, of the powers of the trade unions. If they were to win a referendum – demonstrating that the public had been on the government's side in opposing the militancy of the unions – there would still need to be a framework of measures to kill off their power, and so far the Conservatives had not considered what those measures ought to be.

> There are still people in my party who believe in consensus politics. I regard them as Quislings, as traitors. I mean it.

This was something she had discussed with lawyer friends after a pamphlet had been produced on the subject by the Inns of Court Conservative Society. What concerned her most about trade unionism at this time was the issue of the closed shop. It was anathema to her and her political beliefs. She fiercely defended an individual's right to belong or not to belong to a trade union, and she sought advice on whether she would be able to weaken or even break the power of the closed shop.

Another matter that concerned her arose from a printing-industry dispute that had begun two decades before in July 1958. Some Labour-controlled councils in big cities 'denied normal reporting facilities to journalists working on provincial newspapers involved in the dispute', she says in her memoirs. This 'socialist connivance' with trade-union power did not go down well with the woman who would effectively emasculate the trade unions once she came to power.

A different culture

The issue of immigration came to the fore in early 1978, when Mrs Thatcher gave an interview to television's *World in Action* programme. Discussing the subject, she expressed her concerns that that immigrants themselves might become a victim of a liberal immigration policy. Even earlier immigrants – not just white people – knew that a continuing influx might provoke racist reactions, and these earlier immigrants might themselves become victims: 'People are really rather afraid that this country might be rather swamped by people with a different culture ...' She truly believed that her brand of capitalism was colour-blind. She always declared that individuals should be respected as individuals, regardless of their particular class or race.

> ❝ Standing in the middle of the road is very dangerous; you get knocked down by the traffic from both sides. ❞

Mrs Thatcher felt it was necessary to 'hold out the prospect of an end to immigration, except, of course, for compassionate cases' and to look at the numbers who had a right to enter Britain. However, she added that those who were already here must be treated equally under the law.

She declared herself surprised by the tide of hostility her comments provoked. Labour's Denis Healey said she had used 'cold-blooded calculation in stirring up the muddy waters of racial prejudice', and the home secretary of the time, Merlyn Rees, said she had made racial hatred respectable. She did not back down, however: 'Fifteen years later, this reaction to ideas which were later embodied in legislation and are all but universally accepted seems hysterical.'

She felt only that the response served to show how much politicians had become isolated from people's 'real worries'.

> ❝ We are not in politics to ignore people's worries, we are in politics to deal with them. ❞

'Labour isn't working'

During 1978, the Lib–Lab pact's death knell was sounded by David Steel. It would, he announced, come to an end after the current parliamentary session.

During the summer, the Tories' famous – some would say infamous – poster campaign began with a slogan that is remembered even now as one of the most straightforward yet brutal slogans in politics: 'Labour isn't working'.

It was a poster dreamed up by the ad agency Saatchi & Saatchi – their first campaign for the Tories – and the posters showed huge queues of jobless. (It was an image that would come back to haunt the Saatchi brothers when the Tories dismissed them: a newspaper cartoon reproduced the 'Labour isn't working' poster, but plonked the brothers, looking miserable and dejected, right at the back of the queue!)

On 7 September James Callaghan, now Prime Minister, announced that there would be no autumn election, surprising many, even in his own party. It seems likely that the heavy-hitting advertising campaign was largely responsible for Callaghan's decision to wait until the following year.

Winter was approaching, however. Industrial unrest was becoming a part of everyday life. This particular winter would be one that Callaghan would remember as the one that ushered in the cold snows of a political wilderness for Labour. It was also given a name: the Winter of Discontent.

A terrorist bomb

That sobriquet was, of course, taken from Shakespeare's *Richard III*, and Gloucester's immortal lines that open the play: 'Now is the winter of our discontent / Made glorious summer by this sun of York ...' James Callaghan himself used the phrase in a TV interview in February 1979, when he said, 'I had known it was going to be a "winter of discontent".' The phrase subsequently appeared in newspapers – the *Telegraph* on 9 February and in a *Sun* headline on 30 April.

Margaret Thatcher, of course, believed that the Tories would have triumphed even had Callaghan not delayed the general election from the previous year: 'I believe that we might have scraped in with a small overall majority.' Nevertheless, there is little doubt that this winter was decisive in firmly ushering Labour out of power and making the advent of a Thatcher government an inevitability. There would be no sun to make a glorious summer for Labour in 1979.

The Winter of Discontent was a season of heavy snow, gales and floods. The chill was evident, too, in the attitudes of the trade unions: weary of incomes policies, they were in no mood to be tamed. Both the Wilson and Callaghan governments had tried to work with the unions to bring about social and economic policies that would be acceptable to everyone. After a series of wrangles, the government unilaterally imposed its own income targets of 10 per cent for the years 1977–8 and 5 per cent for 1978–9. The trade unions saw these as far too restrictive, and a huge wave of strikes rocked the country throughout both Wilson's and Callaghan's administrations.

One of the most unpopular union actions was that by local authority workers and those in the National Health Service. They rejected the 5 per cent pay limit imposed on them, and said they would be on strike in the New Year.

Lorry drivers, too, were called out on strike by the powerful Transport and General Workers' Union in January. They had been demanding a 25 per cent rise in pay. About two million workers faced being laid off as a result.

Newspaper headlines screamed of hospital patients – including the terminally ill – who were not receiving the treatment they should decently be getting; of corpses stored in overflowing mortuaries because gravediggers in Liverpool were on strike; of the growing pile of rubbish in London's Leicester Square.

Mrs Thatcher herself later acknowledged how crucial these years would prove to be in the future fortunes of the Conservative Party:

'Appalling as the scenes of the winter of 1978/79 turned out to be, without them and without their exposure of the true nature of socialism, it would have been far more difficult to achieve what was done in the 1980s.'

During January 1979, Thatcher was once again to be seen on *Weekend World*, suggesting union reforms. On the

14th, she offered to cooperate in any legislation the Callaghan government might wish to introduce to outlaw secondary picketing and establish no-strike agreements for essential services. However, the government, while making no direct reply, did ease pay guidelines and lorry drivers ended their strikes locally.

March of 1979 spelled both great victory and great sadness for Mrs Thatcher. On 28 March, Callaghan's government was defeated in a confidence vote and a general election was consequently forced. However, just two days later, Margaret Thatcher experienced a personal tragedy.

She was attending a fundraising function in her constituency, and was also due to make a Party Election Broadcast that evening – something that was very much on her mind when her press officer, Derek Howe, approached her. He explained that there had been an explosion in the House of Commons precincts and that someone had been seriously hurt.

'A hundred possibilities – though not the correct one – went through my mind as we drove down to the BBC studios in Portland Place,' says Mrs Thatcher in *The Path to Power*. Before she went to be made up for the programme, a producer took her to a private room and told her it was her campaign manager and close friend Airey Neave who had been hurt – critically. It had been the work of an IRA breakaway faction called the Irish National Liberation Army, who had put a bomb under Neave's car and it had gone off as he drove up the ramp from the House of Commons car park.

'It was very unlikely,' she writes, 'that he would survive – indeed, by the time I heard the news he may well have been dead.'

Mrs Thatcher could not go on with the election broadcast after that. She phoned the Prime Minister and explained. She felt not only very stunned but also very bitter that 'this man – my friend – who had shrugged off so much danger in his life should be murdered by someone worse than a common criminal'. She would never forget the incident, and it served only to toughen her already hardline attitude towards all terrorists: an attitude which would prove decisive in her later handling of such events as the Brighton bombing and the siege of the Iranian Embassy.

Preparations for the general election continued, however, and Mrs Thatcher knew that her own image was vital if she were to sell herself and her party to the nation. She employed a former television producer, Gordon Reece – the man who was also responsible for bringing in the Saatchis to run the Tories' advertising campaign – to help her cultivate it. He coached her to lower her voice, to avoid the stridency to which she was sometimes prone, and offered her advice on her clothes and hairstyle. She worked as hard as always on the campaign trail, making endless public appearances and speeches. It was clear that the writing was on the wall for the Labour government.

Victory for the Tories on 3 May led Mrs Thatcher to the doors of Number 10, and the next day she was announced as Britain's first woman prime minister.

THE END OF WINTER:
Margaret Steps into the Sunshine

❛ I don't mind how much my ministers talk – as long as they do what I say. ❜

On 5 May, Margaret Thatcher announced her first Cabinet. Geoffrey Howe became Chancellor of the Exchequer, Jim Prior was put in charge of employment, Lord (Peter) Carrington went to the Foreign Office, and Mark Carlisle inherited Mrs Thatcher's old portfolio, education.

Before entering Number 10 the previous day, someone had asked her if she had any thoughts about Emmeline Pankhurst, the leader of the militant wing of the women's suffrage movement in Edwardian Britain, and about her own father, Alf Roberts. Unsurprisingly for a woman never known for embracing women's rights as an issue, she ignored the question of the suffragette entirely, concentrating instead on her father:

❛He brought me up to believe all the things I do believe, and they are just the values on which I've fought the election. And it's passionately interesting to me that the things that I learned in a small town in a very modest home are just the things that I believe have won the election. ❜

Although she had just won a general election, Margaret Thatcher's position at this stage was still far from secure. There was very much a feeling that Labour had lost rather than the Tories had won. Opinion polls suggested that the Conservative leader was unpopular with the general public, while many in her own party found the idea of serving under a woman leader hard to stomach. Nevertheless, her will to succeed had brought her this far, and would take her a great deal further. On 15 May Mrs Thatcher was making her first sallies against the Opposition as Prime Minister. One MP asked why 'choice' and 'diversity' should be 'dirty words', and Mrs Thatcher was quick to answer the question:

There is nothing whatever wrong with choice and diversity. They are central to Conservative policies and are precisely what Britain wants and needs … Far from stamping out enterprise and opportunity, we shall foster and increase them because we know that without them the economy will wither and die.

As time went on, she soon warmed to her vision of what Conservatism stood for, in particular to what would become one of the main planks of her government's policy: privatization. In 1981 Cable & Wireless was privatized, followed swiftly by Amersham International, Britoil and Enterprise Oil. In the later years of her leadership, as her free market economic policies gathered momentum, such diverse industries as British Telecom, British Gas, British Airways and regional water companies would all be nationalized.

'The conscientious citizen under the Labour government was not getting a fair deal,' she told the house. 'People would not achieve their ambition of home ownership from a government dedicated to extending their powers over citizens' lives; "public ownership" was a misnomer, because the public did not own any of the nationalized industries and could not get at those who ran them. People realized that they got a better deal from competition than from state monopoly; that Britain's economic decline had something to do with the fact that the skilled did not get fair differentials and the exceptionally talented were not allowed fair rewards; and that the full magnitude of our decline had been concealed by North Sea oil. They also knew that the unfortunate members of society cannot be sufficiently helped unless opportunities are given to the able.

'The choice before the people was to take further strides in the direction of the corporatist all-powerful state or to restore the balance in favour of the individual. The Labour Party stood for the former. We offered the latter. The difference is clear-cut, and we steadily put it across during the campaign. It was indeed a watershed election. The result was decisive, with a difference of about two million votes between the two major parties, which was the largest difference since 1935.'

Another terrorist bomb

Foreign travel took up much of the new prime minister's first few months in office, as it would do throughout her tenure. After the June European elections showed heavy Conservative gains, Mrs Thatcher attended her first EC summit in Strasbourg on the 21st, and on the 26th she was at her first G7 summit in Tokyo. In July, she was in Lusaka with Lord Carrington to discuss the future of Zimbabwe, which was then called Rhodesia.

> If one leads a country such as Britain – a strong country that has taken a lead in world affairs in good times and bad, that is always reliable – then you must have a touch of iron about you.

In August 1979, Earl Mountbatten of Burma was killed, along with three other people, when an IRA bomb blew up his fishing boat in Donegal Bay, near his home in County Sligo. On 5 September, Mrs Thatcher and Lord Carrington were meeting the Irish premier at Number 10 to discuss Mountbatten's murder.

Rhodesia was back on the agenda later that month, when the dynamic duo of Margaret Thatcher and Carrington opened the Lancaster House summit on the southern African country's future. The Rhodesian settlement took a lot of Mrs Thatcher's time during the following months. The so-called Lancaster House agreement, which gave the country its independence, was signed in December, and was viewed as a triumph for the pair.

In February 1980 there were free elections, and Robert Mugabe and his Zimbabwe African National Union (ZANU-PF) won a landslide victory. Independence finally came on 17 April.

However, Rhodesia – while one of the most important issues of the period – was not the only aspect of foreign affairs that occupied Margaret Thatcher's time. During the latter part of 1979 she had met the Chinese premier, Hua Guofeng, who visited London on 28 October; she had flown to Bonn for a summit with Helmut Schmidt, the West German chancellor; an Anglo-French summit had been held at Number 10; an EEC summit was held in Dublin in November, at which Mrs Thatcher famously banged the table and demanded, 'I want my money back!' This was her dramatic attempt to renegotiate Britain's contribution to the EEC budget.

In December, she was in Washington for another summit meeting – this time with President Jimmy Carter.

The following year – less than a year after the terrorist murder of Airey Neave – came yet another major terrorist incident.

The Iranian Embassy siege

Margaret Thatcher's ability to handle the unpredictability and life-or-death reality of terrorism was put to the test in

May 1980 when a group of gunmen who belonged to an organization calling itself 'the Group of the Martyr' forced their way into the Iranian Embassy in London and took twenty-six hostages. They were Iranian Arabs from Arabistan, who had been trained in Iraq and were opposed to the regime in Iran. Most of the hostages were Iranian staff, but there was also a policeman who had been on duty outside and two journalists from the BBC who had been in the embassy making visa applications.

The gunmen had a list of ninety-one prisoners whom they wanted the Iranian government to set free. They were also demanding that the rights of Iranian dissidents be recognized and that an aircraft be laid on to take them and their hostages out of the UK.

Writing later about the incident in her memoirs, Mrs Thatcher felt her approach to dealing with it was clear:

> ‘My policy would be to do everything possible to resolve the crisis peacefully, without unnecessarily risking the lives of the hostages, but above all to ensure that terrorism should be – and be seen to be – defeated.’

The Home Secretary at the time, William Whitelaw, kept Mrs Thatcher informed of events, while, at the same time, the Metropolitan Police were keeping up communications with the terrorists via a specially laid telephone line. Patient negotiation was Mrs Thatcher's first recourse.

That weekend, while the hostage situation was still

in progress, Mrs Thatcher was at Chequers in Buckinghamshire, the country residence of serving British prime ministers. At that stage, however, the position in London began to deteriorate rapidly, despite the release of a few of the hostages, and she was called back early to the capital. By 5 May – the sixth day of the siege – the gunmen were becoming very frustrated because their demands had not been met. There were threats and more threats, and finally they executed a hostage. The body of Abbas Lavasani was pushed out of the embassy at about 5 p.m.

As Mrs Thatcher sped back to London she received an urgent call from William Whitelaw, her deputy in this matter. He advised her that the lives of the other hostages were now at even greater risk and requested her permission to send in the SAS.

'Yes, go in,' she said, before ordering the car back onto the road to complete its journey to London. It seemed a long drive back as she agonized over what might be happening now that Operation Nimrod had been launched.

The surprise assault by the SAS was carried out with clinical efficiency and under the glare of the world's media. Nineteen hostages were rescued, five gunmen were killed and one was taken prisoner. None of them managed to escape. Most importantly, especially in terms of vindicating Margaret Thatcher's decision to take drastic action, there were no casualties among police or SAS. She declared that their behaviour made everyone 'proud to be British'.

Relieved that her gamble had paid off, Mrs Thatcher wanted to congratulate the SAS men and went to the

Regent's Park barracks to do so. There, she was met by the SAS commander, Peter de la Billière. She was able to see what had happened as it was replayed on television news, and was treated to a running commentary from the men, with occasional relieved laughter acting as punctuation. One of the men turned to her and said, 'We never thought you'd let us do it.'

In later years questions were raised about the killing of so many of the gunmen, with some hostages reporting that some of the terrorists had thrown down their weapons before being shot. At the time, however, the episode was viewed as a resounding success for Mrs Thatcher and for anti-terrorism alike.

> ⁶Britain had sent a signal to terrorists everywhere: there would be no deals, and no favours extorted by terrorism.⁷

'The lady's not for turning'

Mrs Thatcher was soon back on the international circuit once again. Only days after the successful storming of the besieged embassy, she was at the funeral in Belgrade of Josip Broz Tito, the Yugoslavian President, who had established a communist state independent of the USSR after the Second World War. Then, in June, she was off to an EC summit in Venice, followed by a G7 summit there later in the month.

THE END OF WINTER

❛ I owe nothing to Women's Lib. ❜

Four months later came the Conservative Party conference in Brighton, at which the efforts of her speechwriter, Ronnie Millar, were rewarded with much laughter and applause. It was the speech that contained one of her most memorable lines. She rose at 2.30 p.m. on 10 October to make her speech to the Brighton gathering. Her strategy for dealing with the inherent problems in Britain's economy was producing, as she had anticipated, short-term hardships. She spoke of unemployment (rising), the recession (deepening), inflation (higher than expected). The government's economic strategy was proving to be a tough one for the public to swallow, but she believed it was right. She also perceived a lack of public understanding in what the party were trying to do. However, she would not be persuaded to alter course.

❛To those waiting with bated breath for that favourite media catchphrase, the "U-turn," I have one thing to say. "You turn if you want to. [Much laughter.] The lady's not for turning." [More laughter and applause.] I say that not only to you, but to our friends overseas, and also to those who are not our friends.❜

The message was directed as much to cabinet colleagues as to anyone else. She knew that there were still many powerful players in her own party who opposed the increasingly right-wing and laissez-faire direction in which her long-term policies were heading. Nevertheless, she would not be deflected. She was keen to emphasize that her political goals would always transcend issues of popularity.

❛ If you just set out to be liked, you would be prepared to compromise on anything at any time, and you would achieve nothing. ❜

A special relationship

In November 1980, Ronald Reagan was elected as the fortieth President of the United States. Mrs Thatcher had got on with his predecessor Jimmy Carter well enough – though he had certainly found her formidable, remarking to one of his aides after one meeting that it was 'the first time that I've given someone forty-five minutes and only managed to speak for five minutes myself' – but the closeness of the relationship between her and Ronald Reagan became a symbol of the 'special relationship' Britain has generally enjoyed with the USA.

❛ It's a pity about Ronnie, he just doesn't understand economics at all. ❜
ON RONALD REAGAN, 1983

Ronald Reagan shared Mrs Thatcher's deep and abiding distrust of anything collective and her love of individualism, as she explained to the National Press Club in Washington, DC, in June 1995:

 Both Ronald Reagan and I deliberately set out to reverse state control, liberate individual initiative and stand up to a Soviet Empire which was every bit as evil as he described it – and a great deal more serious threat to our way of life than today's revisionists pretend. His main task lay in foreign and defence policy – which was only natural for a superpower. My main task was in economic affairs – to roll back collectivism in all its forms. This included, of course, a campaign against communism everywhere – the most total tyranny in the world.

President Reagan very much reciprocated Margaret Thatcher's admiration, and felt that they had a great deal in common. Like her, he could 'boast' humble beginnings. He had been born above a shop, as she was, but in his case his father's business was selling shoes in Tampico, Illinois. As an actor, he was noted for starring in B-movies, and, when his acting career began to slow up in the post-war years, his interest in politics grew. He was originally a Democrat and was an admirer of Franklin Roosevelt. He also served as president of the Screen Actors' Guild for some years. However, he became concerned over the communism he perceived in his union, and became more conservative, eventually joining the Republicans in 1962.

Reagan's election pleased Mrs Thatcher as something of 'immediate and fundamental importance', she says in *The Downing Street Years*. The USA, she says, was 'the greatest force for liberty that the world has known'. She had met him twice while she was in opposition and he was governor of California. Now she was sending him warm congratulations on his election victory, and inviting him to visit Britain soon.

In February she was off to Washington D.C. to meet the new president of the United States.

> ❮ I am an ally of the United States. We believe the same things, we believe passionately in the same battle of ideas, we will defend them to the hilt. ❯

Riots

1981 was the year of riots. They first broke out in Brixton, London, in April. Police officers and members of the public were hurt, shops were looted, cars were destroyed and 215 people were arrested. Three months later, it was the turn of Southall – also in London – and Toxteth in Liverpool. They were sparked off by a very complex set of issues, but it cannot be denied that the unpopularity of Margaret Thatcher's government, as well as her attitude towards the matter of immigration, had a role to play in their origin.

Riots in Southall began on 3 July when white skinheads

and Asian youths made battle; petrol bombs were thrown; mobs turned on police and even firefighters and ambulance personnel. That weekend saw the riots in Toxteth: looting, arson, attacks on police officers, the dispersal of the mob with CS gas.

(Oh, those poor shopkeepers!)
ON SEEING PICTURES OF THE RIOTS IN TOXTETH, 1981

A week later, rioting broke out in Moss Side, Manchester. It was hoped that community leaders would help to calm matters, but police, who had kept a low profile, now had to move in in large numbers. The Moss Side incidents had been more a case of looting and general hooliganism than a confrontation with the police.

Mrs Thatcher was aware that these riots were 'a godsend' to Labour, however. Critics of the Tory party saw the riots as a symptom of the unemployment and lack of social cohesion engendered by the government's policies. Mrs Thatcher found herself countering these arguments both in the Commons and elsewhere. The phrase 'doctrinaire monetarism' was used again, even by Tories, who said this policy was tugging at the social fabric, tearing it apart.

Mrs Thatcher never accepted these points of view. On the contrary, she was keen to blame left-wing extremists. In *The Downing Street Years,* she argued that riots, hooliganism and crime generally had been rising in Britain since the

1960s – and 'under the very economic policies that our critics were urging us to adopt'. She knew her current economic policies were creating a difficult political environment for her in the short-term, but her legendary stubbornness helped her to weather the storm.

‘ I am extraordinarily patient, provided I get my own way in the end. ’

In the aftermath of the Brixton riots, Mrs Thatcher wanted to know how police handled these tense situations, and asked for a meeting at Scotland Yard. She was shown around and thanked Brixton police officers for their efforts to combat hooliganism and rioting. She had discussions with the then commissioner of the Met, Sir David McNee, and his lieutenants. They told her they wanted to see sentences passed more quickly on offenders instead of after long delays at crown courts. They needed decent riot gear. Mrs Thatcher did not hesitate to promise them action.

In mid-July, she made a similar visit to Toxteth in Liverpool, and remarks in her memoir that the housing in the area 'was by no means the worst in the city'. She talked not only to police, but to councillors and a group of community leaders and young people, who 'talked about their problems with great sincerity'.

She says in her memoir, 'I urged them not to resort to violence or to try to live in separate communities from the rest of us.' As she drove back to London she realized that 'we faced immense problems' in such areas as Toxteth and Brixton. 'People had to find once again a sense of respect for the law, for the neighbourhood, and indeed for themselves,' she writes.

Eventually an inquiry into the riots was set up under Lord Scarman, which was critical of police methods, saying the constabulary had become alienated from parts of the communities it served. Police had also failed to respond to the growing multiculturalism that was now more prevalent in England.

Bitter arguments

On 23 July that year, there was yet more evidence of Cabinet splits on the subject of public expenditure. Spending ministers had put in bids for extra expenditure of more than £6.5 billion, but the Treasury was pushing for less, not more, public spending for 1982–3. Difficult though it was in the current political climate, Mrs Thatcher was determined to push her policy of cutbacks in public spending and consequently found herself embroiled in one of the most bitter arguments on the economy during her time as Prime Minister.

Public spending was far from being the only contentious issue on Margaret Thatcher's agenda. That summer she brought the subject of trade union reform to the fore, and it swiftly caused much Cabinet rancour and infighting. A green paper on trade union immunities had been issued, and comments were due by the end of June.

> ❝ You may have to fight a battle more than once to win it. ❞

When the comments came in, there was evidence of a desire among businesspeople for more radical action to break the power of the trade unions. It was clear that a major reshuffle of her Cabinet was required if Mrs Thatcher was going to be able to take such action. In September, she sought to surround herself with people who were loyal to her personally and who shared her concept of the direction the Conservative Party should take. Men noted for their right-wing tendencies, particularly when it came to matters of the economy, were brought in: Nigel Lawson (a future Chancellor of the Exchequer), Cecil Parkinson and Norman Tebbit. Jim Prior, a former supporter of Edward Heath and a minister noted for his conciliatory attitude towards the trade unions, was moved to Northern Ireland. As an enforceable philosophy, Thatcherism was beginning to take shape.

> ❝ I love argument, I love debate. I don't expect anyone just to sit there and agree with me, that's not their job. ❞

Missing person

Terrorism visited the UK mainland once more, in the shape of an IRA bomb in Chelsea Barracks on 10 October 1981. At the time, Mrs Thatcher was globetrotting, attending several summit meetings, including the North–South summit in Cancun on 21 October and the Anglo-German summit on 18 November.

An embarrassing family problem was an unwelcome visitor less than two months later, when, in January 1982, Mrs Thatcher's son Mark was reported lost in the Sahara. He had been taking part in the Paris–Dakar rally. On television Margaret Thatcher was shown to be visibly upset, as her husband Denis flew out to Dakar. Thatcher Jr was subsequently found, safe and well, some days later.

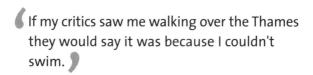

If my critics saw me walking over the Thames they would say it was because I couldn't swim.

This was the year that Conservative fortunes were flagging. However, there was soon to be an international situation that would ensure the party's return to power in the 1983 general election, and give Margaret Thatcher another seven years at Number 10.

A QUESTION OF SOVEREIGNTY:

Margaret Goes to War

> ❝ It is exciting to have a real crisis on your hands, when you have spent half your political life dealing with humdrum issues like the environment. ❞

In November 1998 Carlos Menem, who had been the elected President of Argentina for nine years by that time, visited the United Kingdom. It was the first visit by an Argentine president to the UK since the battle for the Falkland Islands – or Islas Malvinas – in 1982. Peace and reconciliation were the ostensible reasons for the visit, although the question of the sovereignty of the islands was – and still is – very much a sore point.

The wrangle over sovereignty had deep and complex origins. French colonists from St-Malo settled on East Falkland as far back as 1764 (the name 'Malvinas' comes from 'St-Malo'), while the British settled on West Falkland. Spain bought out the French settlement in 1770, and the British left the islands in 1774. Argentina overthrew Spain in 1816 and claimed sovereignty of the islands in 1820. However, Britain took control of the islands just thirteen years later expelling the Argentines, while Argentina continued to lay claim.

There is little doubt that in the event the conflict

provided a much-needed boost to Margaret Thatcher's waning esteem at that time in the eyes of both the British public and other countries. It helped her to victory in the 1983 general election, it consolidated her power within the party, and it is one of the triumphs for which her time as leader is principally remembered. At the time, to the popular mind – bestirred by the populist, demotic, and somewhat oversimplified scribblings of the tabloid press, with headlines that spoke of 'Argie-bargie' – she was a hero. She had gone to war and she had won. Other papers, and other commentators, were more circumspect, and not everyone delighted in the gung-ho bellicosity of the Tory government.

In 1981, the 150th anniversary of the expulsion of the Argentines by the English was approaching, and the new military junta in Argentina put a high priority on the return of the islands to what it considered their rightful ownership.

> ❝ [I]t seems that the imminence of the 150th anniversary was an important factor in the plotting of the Argentine Junta. ❞
> *THE DOWNING STREET YEARS*

The islands' declining population stood at about 1,800, and their economy was flagging. While there was little evidence of strong feeling among British governments over sovereignty – and it had to be said that Britain had not devoted much money to the protection or development of the dependency – there was a reluctance to deny the islanders their self-determination.

However, the junta were determined, and would go to war if necessary. They had set themselves up for an offensive to get the islands back, and autumn 1982 was seen as the possible time for military action. Negotiations in New York in February of that year, to try to reach a diplomatic settlement, had fallen down, and the following month a group of 'scrap dealers' settled on the dependency of South Georgia, south-east of the Falklands, arousing suspicions that this was a precursor to something more permanent. (South Georgia, now a British dependency, was a dependency of the Falkland Islands themselves until 1985.)

Britain sent HMS *Endurance* to remove the so-called scrap dealers, but Argentina saw this as Britain's way of consolidating its hold on the Falkland Islands, and sent an invasion force on 2 April 1982, earlier than it had planned. South Georgia fell to the Argentines the following day. The small permanent garrison of the Falklands, a detachment of Royal Marines, offered resistance until being forced to surrender, and there were conflicting reports about casualties, with an Argentine communiqué later claiming that one of its naval captains had been killed.

'Some reporters said the fighting lasted three hours,' said a report in *The Times* of 3 April, 'and a ham radio operator in the islands reported the invading forces had heavily damaged buildings in Port Stanley [the islands' capital] with machine gun and mortar barrages.'

On the night following the Argentine attack, Britain announced that it was assembling a large naval task force in response to the Argentines' action. At the same time, the Argentine Chargé d'Affaires in London was summoned to the Foreign Office and told he and his staff would have to be out of their offices within four working days, because Britain was breaking off diplomatic relations with Buenos Aires.

> ❛ I know nothing about diplomacy, but I know I want certain things for Britain. ❜

The Argentines had been claiming not only that they had taken South Georgia, but that they had also occupied the Falkland Islands and installed their own government. This was now being confirmed by Mrs Thatcher's Foreign Secretary, Lord Carrington, and by John Nott, the Defence Secretary. Carrington described the Argentines' action as unprovoked aggression. (Carrington later resigned over the issue, saying that, as Foreign Secretary, he should have foreseen the problems, but had failed to do so and to take appropriate action. He remains one of precious few British government ministers who have had the honesty and courage to fall on their swords when faced with failure.)

Mrs Thatcher and her ministers, meanwhile, were busy cancelling engagements so they could remain in readiness to monitor developments. She was to have had a meeting with Dr Richard von Weizsäcker, the chief Burgomaster of West Berlin, who was visiting Britain at the time, but she broke off the meeting and chaired an emergency Cabinet meeting instead.

She had not expected the invasion; no one had. 'The war was very sudden,' she says in *The Downing Street Years*.

❛No one predicted the Argentine invasion more than a few hours in advance, though many predicted it in retrospect. When I became Prime Minister I never thought that I would have to order British troops into combat and I do not think I have ever lived so tensely or intensely as during the whole of that time.❜

In London, the atmosphere was reminiscent of the Second World War. Loudspeaker messages were broadcast at the capital's railway stations and posters were put up telling soldiers from the Third Battalion, the Parachute Regiment, to return to bases immediately. Soon, 28,000 military personnel and a large task force, including two aircraft carriers, were dispatched to the South Atlantic.

One regret Mrs Thatcher voiced at the time – and has repeated since – was the way BBC correspondents behaved. The British government had allowed correspondents on board task force vessels, but the manner in which they reported events was too even-handed for the Iron Lady. She couldn't get her head around the fact that news journalists are supposed to be neutral, and their use of the phrases 'the British' and 'the Argentinians' rather than 'we' and 'us', 'they' and 'them' was beyond her comprehension, which is rather odd for someone who had already had several political years dealing with the media. As a woman brought up to be a fervent patriot, and whose foreign policy always strove to enhance Britain's standing as a nation, she found this use of the third person when talking of our own 'chilling'.

Meanwhile, Britain and the rest of the world were waiting to hear on which side of the fence the USA would eventually stand. After some frantic diplomatic activity by America's Secretary of State Alexander Haig, America came down on the side of the UK. Haig had tried to convince Buenos Aires that, with diplomacy and negotiation, rather than a guarantee of the transfer of sovereignty, Argentina might get what it wanted. But Argentina's President Galtieri was not interested.

As the task force was brought together, Mrs Thatcher addressed the House of Commons on a Saturday. It was, she has said since, one of the most difficult debates she has ever had to open. Some MPs were blaming the government for having failed to foresee what was going to happen. (Some time later, a committee headed by Lord Franks reported that no criticism or blame could be attached to the government 'for the Argentine Junta's decision to commit its act of unprovoked aggression in the invasion of the Falkland Islands on 2 April 1982'.)

'I must tell the house,' Mrs Thatcher said that Saturday morning, 'that the Falkland Islands and their dependencies remain British territory. No aggression and no invasion can alter that simple fact.' It was the objective of the government, she said, to ensure that the islands be freed from occupation and returned to British administration as soon as possible.

> The people of the Falklands Islands, like the people of the United Kingdom, are an island race . . . They are few in number, but they have the right to live in peace, to choose their own way of life and to determine their own allegiance. Their way of life is British: their allegiance is to the crown. It is the wish of the British people and the duty of Her Majesty's Government to do everything that we can to uphold that right. That will be our hope and our endeavour and, I believe, the resolve of every member of the house.

On 7 April, a 200-mile maritime exclusion zone (MEZ) was announced, excluding seagoing craft from the area. Before the month was out, this would be significantly strengthened.

'Just rejoice ...'

By late April, the bulk of the British task force was in place in the South Atlantic, and South Georgia had been retaken. Outside Number 10 Downing Street, Mrs Thatcher delivered one of her most memorable remarks to flashing cameras and baying reporters. First, the Defence Secretary,

John Nott, read a statement, announcing that British troops had landed on South Georgia and had met only limited resistance from the Argentines. A reporter shouted, 'What happens next, Mr Nott? What's your reaction?'

Mrs Thatcher looked out at the assembled reporters, photographers and TV crews. 'Just rejoice at the news,' she told them, 'and congratulate our forces and the Marines.' She turned to walk back into Number 10, saying 'Goodnight' as she did so.

'Are we going to war with Argentina, Mrs Thatcher?' asked another reporter. Mrs Thatcher paused dramatically on the step, turned and said, simply, 'Rejoice!'

On 26 April, the War Cabinet announced a total exclusion zone (TEZ) around the Falklands – the same radius as the maritime exclusion zone announced at the beginning of the month. The total exclusion zone went beyond the maritime exclusion zone announced earlier in the month, in that aircraft as well as seagoing vessels were excluded.

The *Belgrano* is sunk

The runway at Port Stanley was among Argentine positions that British aircraft began to target in an attempt to draw out Argentine naval and air forces.

The most controversial British action during the entire conflict – and one for which Mrs Thatcher has been widely criticized – is the sinking on 2 May 1982 of the 13,644-ton Argentine cruiser *General Belgrano*, which was carrying helicopters and Seacat missiles. Argentina said the ship was leaving the declared combat zone; Britain disagreed, citing the protection of her sailors aboard HMS *Hermes* as justification for the slaughter. HMS *Conqueror*, a nuclear submarine, was ordered to sink *Belgrano*, and did so, killing more than three hundred members of her crew of more than a thousand.

Mrs Thatcher blamed the Argentines themselves for the high death toll. In *The Downing Street Years*, she says that, after the torpedoing of the *Belgrano*, the British submarine moved away as quickly as possible. However, the *Belgrano*'s escorts believed – wrongly, she says – that they would be the next targets, and 'seem to have engaged in anti-submarine activities rather than rescuing its crew, some 321 of whom were lost – though initially the death toll was reported to be much higher. The ship's poor state of battle readiness greatly increased the casualties.'

She has always maintained, in spite of much criticism of the action and a great deal of commentary and analysis to the contrary, that the *Belgrano* was sunk only for military and not political reasons. Rumours to the contrary, she maintains in her memoir, are 'malicious and misleading'.

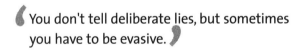

You don't tell deliberate lies, but sometimes you have to be evasive.

There was in the offing a peace initiative from Peru, which some saw as promising. It was said that the British government's decision to sink the *Belgrano* was in an effort to undermine the initiative, but Mrs Thatcher has always claimed that those ministers, including herself, who assembled at Chequers and took the decision to sink the *Belgrano* did not know about the Peruvian proposals.

Mrs Thatcher wanted all-party talks on the Falklands crisis but Michael Foot, then the Labour leader in opposition, refused. Any such consultation among leading politicians would have been on 'Privy Council terms', and this would have entailed secrecy. Foot – after consultations with other senior figures in the Labour Party, including the deputy Labour leader Denis Healey – did not want to compromise his ability to criticize the government if necessary. He had already attacked the timing of the assault on Port Stanley airfield by British aircraft.

Two days after the sinking of the *Belgrano*, HMS *Sheffield* succumbed to attacks from two Argentine Super Etendard jets. The Type 42 destroyer had been hit by a direct hit from an Exocet missile, after another missile had missed its target. *Sheffield* was abandoned and her crew transferred to HMS *Arrow*, while casualties were ferried to the flagship carrier *Hermes*. Twenty-one of Sheffield's crew were killed. It was three days before Sheffield was able to be boarded for towing away, but she listed helplessly in rising seas and eventually sank. This was the first large-scale loss by the British in the conflict.

A Harrier jump jet was also shot down after the *Sheffield* attack, one of a number that had been ordered to bomb airfields on the Falklands. Its pilot, Lieutenant Nicholas Taylor, was killed.

> It is only when you look now and see success that you say that it was good fortune. It was not. We lost 250 of our best young men. I felt every one.

One of the other major episodes in the Falklands conflict was the battle for Goose Green and Darwin. In late April, the Second Battalion, Parachute Regiment, had been deployed to the South Atlantic, and landed on the beaches of San Carlos on 21 May. Goose Green and Darwin were Argentine-occupied settlements and were seen as a threat to the flank of the British advance towards Port Stanley. During the ensuing battle, seventeen British and 250 Argentine soldiers lost their lives; a further 1,400 Argentines were taken prisoner, many of them ill-equipped conscripts. It was eight weeks to the day since Argentina had launched its attack on the Falklands.

The Argentines kept up their resistance with spasmodic but often fierce fire, but it was a combination of infantry attacks and artillery bombardment that eventually defeated them, when the British took the high ground around Port Stanley. The Argentines surrendered on 14 June. The ruling junta resigned, and the Falklands remain a British colony. On 16 June, the *Guardian* leader began with the words:

> A thousand dead, terrible wounds; the Union Jack flying again over the Falklands (pop. 1,800);

rejoicing and mutual congratulation in the House of Commons; champagne and Rule Britannia in Downing Street – each must draw his or her own balance sheet and historians must decide where to place the Falklands War in the annals of Britain's post-1945 adjustment to her reduced circumstances as a declining power.'

On 3 July, Mrs Thatcher made a speech in Cheltenham, when she defined what she called the 'Falklands spirit':

'We have ceased to be a nation in retreat. We have instead a newfound confidence – born in the economic battles at home and tested and found true eight thousand miles away . . . And so today we can rejoice at our success in the Falklands and take pride in the achievements of the men and women of our task force. But we do so not as at some flickering of a flame which must seen be dead: no, we rejoice that Britain has rekindled that spirit which has fired her for generations past, and which today has begun to burn as brightly as before.'

THE BATTLE FOR THE PITS:

Margaret Takes On King Coal

❛ Britain could not be made ungovernable by the Fascist Left. ❜

The rest of 1982 saw Margaret Thatcher again visiting several countries, taking in a twelve-day tour of the Far East (visiting Japan, China and Hong Kong), dropping in on the new German Chancellor, Helmut Kohl, and attending a summit in Copenhagen. In January 1983, she and her husband Denis secretly spent a few days in the Falkland Islands.

Also in that month, she once again reshuffled her Cabinet, substituting Michael Heseltine for John Nott as Defence Secretary. In May, she called a general election for 9 June, causing her to cut short her attendance at the G7 summit in Williamsburg so that she could campaign.

On election day, the Thatcher government was returned with a majority of 144 seats, and the new Cabinet saw Geoffrey Howe moving to the Foreign Office, while Leon Brittan became Home Secretary. Nigel Lawson became Chancellor of the Exchequer and had not been in the job more than a few weeks when he announced a step forward in terms of Mrs Thatcher's economic goals: public expenditure cuts of £500 million.

In October, Cecil Parkinson – who had been

appointed as Tory Chairman in 1981 – caused a major embarrassment for the party which had at various stages in its history tried to sell itself as representative of 'family values'. Parkinson had been instrumental in the Tories' success in the 1983 general election, before which he had been a close confidant of Mrs Thatcher during the Falklands crisis. His future in the Tory government seemed secure. His affair with his secretary, Sara Keays – who became pregnant by him – proved to be his undoing, however. Margaret Thatcher urged him to remain with his wife and refused to ask for his resignation, even when the matter became public. It was only when it became clear that the matter was not going to die down quickly that she accepted his resignation from the Cabinet and the chairmanship. She had proved herself to be a loyal colleague in this case, but at the expense of undermining some of her party's much-vaunted Victorian values.

Nevertheless, as is the case with so many politicians who find themselves disgraced, Parkinson was able to bounce back once any residual ignominy had left the minds of a fickle public, and he would return to the Conservative cabinet to serve as Energy Secretary and Transport Secretary. The episode would come back to haunt him eighteen years later, when it transpired that he had unceremoniously dumped his daughter, Flora, after her birth, and she had been brought up by her mother, Sara, who had seen her through many childhood difficulties. It further emerged that Parkinson had put a legal gag on anything to do with his daughter, effectively stifling any possible examination of his questionable morals in the media.

Writing in the *Guardian* in January 2002, Simon Hoggart had this to say about Cecil (now Lord) Parkinson:

> It's hard for any of us to find excuses for the ferocious legal injunctions he obtained and which lapsed only this month. These not only shielded Flora, and so himself, from unwelcome scrutiny, but according to Sara prevented her from writing to her MP or councillor about the girl's education, and even kept her out of her school photographs. To decide to ignore her is one thing; to create the illusion that she did not exist is another.

'Mr Scargill's insurrection'

Two major episodes in Margaret Thatcher's premiership occurred during 1984. The second was her survival of an IRA attempt on her life, which will be addressed in the next chapter. The first was the miners' strike, and it would prove to be a bloody and controversial affair, with face and dignity lost on both sides, but with Mrs Thatcher being seen once again as the ruthless enemy of anything that smacked of collectivism. This loathing fuelled her determination to smash the unions, and the miners were in her line of fire.

The miners' strike was one of the longest and bitterest

industrial disputes in Britain this side of the Second World War, and lasted a year – a year that saw picket-line violence and clashes with police, but also mining communities standing solidly behind the pitmen as they fought for the future of Britain's coal mines, for their livelihoods and for their dignity.

> To cure the British disease with socialism was like trying to cure leukaemia with leeches.

A largely right-wing press, however, led by tabloids such as the *Sun* and the *Daily Mail*, helped to ensure that public sympathy went against the miners. Some miners went against the NUM, too, during that bitter year, and formed the Union of Democratic Mineworkers.

The strike began at the beginning of March, and Mrs Thatcher was determined not to surrender, as she saw it, to the president of the National Union of Mineworkers (NUM), Arthur Scargill.

Scargill had been in coal mining all his life. He had been an apprentice at Woolley Colliery in Yorkshire in 1953, and by 1964 had become a colliery delegate on his local branch committee of the NUM. He organized the mass picket of the Saltley Gate coke works near Birmingham in 1972. When the miners helped to bring down the Heath government two years later, Scargill was already the Yorkshire area NUM president. To become the NUM national president in 1981, he succeeded in claiming more than 70 per cent of the vote.

He organized the strike by calling ballots at individual collieries, rather than risk losing a national vote. Later in the action, Scargill did not do himself any favours in the eyes of most of the public when he asked Colonel Gaddafy, the Libyan leader, to help finance the strike, when a British policewoman, Yvonne Fletcher, had been shot dead outside the Libyan Embassy in London by one of the country's agents. Scargill also took loans from other unions, without proper discussions, it was said, with the TUC.

For Mrs Thatcher, the power of the trade unions had always been one of the least acceptable aspects of the socialism she so distrusted. She viewed the miners' leaders largely as communists who sought to introduce 'dark, divisive clouds of Marxist Socialism'.

> ❮ I had never had any doubt about the true aim of the hard Left: they were revolutionaries who sought to impose a Marxist system on Britain whatever the means and whatever the cost. ❯

She saw the 'hard left' as being entrenched in three institutions: the Labour Party, local government and trade unions – her attitude no doubt found its origins in her father's own distaste of collectivism, as well as in the experiences of recent governments whose power was paralysed by widespread strikes. The Left's 'attack', as she saw it, was coming from the NUM, who 'were destined to provide the shock troops'. Mrs Thatcher well remembered the strike of 1973–4 which had all but destroyed Ted Heath's government of the time, and recognized that the NUM was similarly capable of making or breaking her government. It was something she sought to avoid at all costs.

Nigel Lawson, who had become Energy Secretary in September 1981, had already begun to build up stocks of coal so that the country could withstand a miners' strike. These stocks were available at power stations and not just at pits, where a miners' picket line might prevent the fuel from being taken away for use.

Even in the most dark and difficult days of the strike, Margaret Thatcher resolutely refused to countenance any negotiations with the miners. 'Beer and sandwiches at No. 10? No, never,' she declared. During the course of the strike, miners gradually drifted back to work and she sung their praises: 'Scabs? They are lions!' The NUM eventually conceded defeat. Margaret Thatcher was then able to do what she had set out to do, which the miners had struggled to prevent them from doing: to dismantle the coal industry. In 1985, there were around 200,000 people employed in the industry; by 1995, it was down to just 11,000, and many once-thriving, vibrant mining communities have been destroyed as a result.

One incident that was seen as a turning point was a riot at Orgreave coking works in South Yorkshire in May. Thousands of miners had tried to prevent supplies from leaving for the Scunthorpe British Steel plant. At one point, Scargill, then forty-six, was arrested while leading a column of pickets to the coke works. Police had told them they could go no further. 'No way, no way!' said Scargill, but after some exchanges of words he was arrested. Later, he was released on unconditional bail by Rotherham magistrates. He had pleaded not guilty to obstruction charges.

'I will continue to do my job leading the miners on the picket lines at Orgreave,' he told reporters. This was seen as his way of refusing to take part in peace talks with the National Coal Board.

'For the second day running, police in riot gear carrying shields cleared a way for convoys of lorries to take coking coal to the BSC [British Steel Corporation] plant despite a barrage of missiles from about 3,000 pickets,' reported *The Times* of 31 May 1984.

Mrs Thatcher lost little time in making political capital out of the situation as the strike continued to crumble, and 1984 gave way to 1985. In the Commons, she goaded the then Labour leader Neil Kinnock, and made reference to the Orgreave incident, now several months in the past:

❝Throughout the strike the right honourable gentleman [Kinnock] has had the choice between standing up to the NUM leadership and keeping silent. He has kept silent. When the leadership of the NUM called a strike without a ballot, in defiance of union rules, the right honourable gentleman stayed silent. When pickets tried by violence to close down pits in Nottinghamshire and elsewhere, against the democratically expressed wishes of the local miners, the right honourable gentleman stayed silent. When the NUM tried to impose mob rule at Orgreave, the right honourable gentleman stayed silent. Only when the general secretary of the TUC had the courage to tell the leadership of the NUM that its tactics were unacceptable did the right honourable gentleman take on the role of Little Sir Echo ... I challenge the leader of the Opposition. Will he urge the NUM to accept that agreement or will he not?

MPs shouted, 'Answer, answer!' but Kinnock did not. Mrs Thatcher's stinging response was, 'He will not answer because he dare not answer.'

The dispute, Mrs Thatcher maintains in her memoirs, had been totally unnecessary. It was unreasonable of the NUM, she said, to oppose plans to close uneconomic pits. It was, she says in *The Downing Street Years*, not a strike about uneconomic pits: it was a political strike and for her its result was decisive:

What the strike's defeat established was that Britain could not be made ungovernable by the Fascist Left. Marxists wanted to defy the law of the land in order to defy the laws of economics.

BRAVERY IN BRIGHTON:

Margaret Survives the Assassin's Bomb

> ❝ It was clearly an attempt not only to disrupt and terminate our conference; it was an attempt to cripple Her Majesty's democratically elected Government. That is the scale of the outrage we have all shared, and the fact that we are gathered here now, shocked but composed, is a sign not only that this attack has failed but that all attempts to destroy democracy by terrorism will fail. ❞

Mrs Thatcher clearly viewed the miners' strike as a major victory for her government. The forces of Evil (Marxism) had been defeated by the forces of Good (a Conservative government). However, the pits had not been the only things on her mind. In November 1984 she had been to India to attend the funeral of the assassinated Prime Minister, Indira Gandhi, a friend and one of the few women she ever regarded as a mentor. And three days later, no doubt to Mrs Thatcher's immense relief, Ronald Reagan had been re-elected US President.

In keeping with her pursuit of right-wing economic policies, in particular her belief that the free market is the only way to run an economy – even with what we might term 'natural' monopolies, such as telecoms, nationwide transport systems and utilities – Mrs Thatcher's government floated the hitherto publicly owned British Telecom. It was the Tory government's first major privatization.

Later that month, the House of Lords upheld a ban on trade unions at GCHQ (Government Communications Headquarters), the spy base in Cheltenham that monitors global electronic transmissions. This move, instigated by Mrs Thatcher, was another blow to trade unionism in Britain, and it would be several years before a Labour government came to power – albeit of the 'New' variety – and allowed trade unions to organize there once again.

Nevertheless, the month of October 1984, while the miners' strike was still filling column inches of newsprint, was noted for the attempt on Margaret Thatcher's life by the Provisional IRA. They blew up part of the Grand Hotel in Brighton, where ministers, top party members and other delegates to the Conservative Party conference were staying.

Mrs Thatcher was in her suite with Robin Butler, her principal private secretary, in the early hours of the morning, still working on official papers. They heard a thud, which shook the room, followed by the different noise of falling masonry. By now, glass from the window of her sitting room was strewn across the carpet. She knew at once that there had been a bomb, but thought at first that it might have been a car bomb in the street below.

Tons of rubble hurtled through seven floors of the hotel, killing the Conservative MP for Enfield South, Sir Anthony Berry, and Roberta Wakeham, wife of the

Government Chief Whip, John Wakeham. Wakeham himself and the Industry Secretary, Norman Tebbit, were trapped in the rubble. Both men needed operations. Wakeham suffered serious leg injuries. Tebbit had been found when his protruding foot was spotted after about two hours.

Mrs Thatcher had left her bathroom just two minutes before it was severely damaged in the blast, but, had she still been in the bathroom, 'the worst I would have suffered … were minor cuts. Those who had sought to kill me had placed the bomb in the wrong place,' she says in *The Downing Street Years*. Her account continues:

> The lights, thankfully, remained on: the importance of this played on my mind for some time and for months afterwards I always kept a torch by my bed when I was staying the night in a strange house.

Even after she had checked on her staff (one had received an electric shock from a photocopier, but otherwise they were all unhurt) and had put a copy of her speech for the following day into her briefcase, she reflected for a moment on what could have been, and what might yet be. From her memoirs:

> There is always a fear of a second device, carefully timed to catch and kill those fleeing from the first explosion. It was also necessary for them to find a way out of the hotel which was both unblocked and safe.

Forty-year-old Ron Farley, Tory group leader of Bradford City Council, had been in the hotel bar when the bomb had gone off, still in evening dress. He told the *Guardian* that everyone had been showered with glass and he had told them to get down. 'I shouted to the people to join hands. There were about thirty or forty of us who linked up and we slowly made our way through the back. There was one policeman lying on the floor, covered in rubble. We pulled away all the rubbish. He was injured, I don't know how badly. Then I found this poor old dear, a seventy-year-old lady, can you believe? She had one eye missing. It was terrible.'

The Tory party organizer, Harvey Thomas, was full of praise for the firefighters: 'They worked for an hour, during which time we were freezing cold and the water was pouring over us. I had been on the seventh floor and I was pulled out of the fifth so I must have fallen two floors.'

Mrs Thatcher and her entourage – having been led out of the hotel by the back door, stepping over rubble, their clothes turned grey-white by masonry dust – went to the police station and were given tea in the chief constable's room. John Gummer and Geoffrey Howe, both ministers, were there with her, as was Leon Brittan, then Home Secretary. No one knew at this stage whether the conference would continue. Had the conference centre itself taken a hit? There was talk of her returning to Number 10, but Mrs Thatcher was determined not only to stay, but to give her speech to the conference the following day.

Margaret, Denis and her detectives spent the rest of the night at the police college, where rooms were waiting for them. She slept only fitfully, and awoke to the sounds of the preparation of breakfast – only to learn on the morning news of the deaths of Roberta Wakeham and Anthony Berry. As they had left the hotel only a few hours before, it had not previously occurred to her that people might have been killed.

When she got to the conference room, she discovered that many people who had been in the hotel the previous night had lost most of their clothes, and the local branch of Marks & Spencer had opened especially to kit them out.

The first debate was, appropriately, on Northern Ireland. Mrs Thatcher remained to listen, but then went off to work on her speech, which would now have to be radically revised. Much of the Labour-bashing part of her speech was removed. This was not a time, she decided, for partisan gibes. She delivered the speech from paper rather than use an autocue, as she had intended, and ad-libbed much of what she said.

❛The bomb attack on the Grand Hotel early this morning was first and foremost an inhuman, undiscriminating attempt to massacre innocent unsuspecting men and women staying in Brighton for our Conservative conference. ❜

There was speculation about the size of the bomb. Some experts said it was only about ten or fifteen pounds. While the dead and critically injured were still trapped in the rubble, the Provisional IRA in Dublin issued a statement claiming responsibility and saying the bomb was one hundred pounds.

The Provos had this message for the Prime Minister: 'Today we were unlucky, but remember we only have to be lucky once. You will have to be lucky always. Give Ireland peace and there will be no war.'

After the speech, she went to the Royal Sussex Hospital and spent two hours talking to the injured. She spoke to eighteen people, after which she said she would not give in to the IRA. Some of the victims had been asleep when the bomb went off.

In *The Downing Street Years*, she describes her feelings about the visit:

❨ I left the hospital overcome by such bravery and suffering … As I spent that night in what had become my home I could not stop thinking about those unable to return to theirs. ❩

There had been close personal protection surrounding Mrs Thatcher and her colleagues for about two months, since a tip-off about a possible IRA assassination attempt. Three Special Branch officers were assigned to guard the Prime Minister personally, while other protection officers were stationed on the first-, second- and third-floor landings.

The tip-off had come from the FBI, who warned that an IRA sleeper unit had been activated. Extra weight had been lent to this tip-off a couple of weeks before the blast, when five alleged IRA gunrunners had been arrested and the trawler *Marita Anne* had been captured off the Irish coast.

The Regency building was a strong one, and seemed to have absorbed much of the blast. This, anyway, was the speculation among experts, who seemed initially amazed that the bomb had not claimed more lives and created more devastation.

Mrs Thatcher always maintained that there was no excuse for the IRA's terror campaign. It was not, as many would blithely describe it, 'mindless', but a calculated campaign of terror and violence – and the threat of violence – in order to achieve political ends. She recognized that there were terrorists on both sides of the Northern Ireland question, and abhorred the fact that too many people were prepared to give them support. She nevertheless viewed the nationalist side as the real problem, avowing in *The Downing Street Years* that the IRA 'are the core of the terrorist problem', and that their Protestant counterparts 'would probably disappear if the IRA could be beaten'.

The news of the Brighton bombing was deeply disturbing not just for Mrs Thatcher and her party, but for the country as a whole. It will go down in history as just that kind of shocking incident, along with events such as the assassination of John F. Kennedy in 1963 and the attack on the World Trade Center in New York nearly forty years later, that made a deep impression in people's minds.

On 28 August 1986, Margaret Thatcher and Norman Tebbit returned to the Grand Hotel to attend its reopening, nearly two years after the explosion that might have claimed both their lives.

TARZAN AND THE FLYING MACHINES:

Rifts in Margaret's Cabinet

❛ ... whereas with me it is certain political principles that provide a reference point and inner strength, for Michael [Heseltine] such things are unnecessary. His own overwhelming belief in himself is sufficient. ❜

Mikhail Gorbachev was a man Margaret Thatcher could 'do business with'. She had said as much on the occasion of a visit by him and his wife Raisa to Chequers in December 1984. The couple made quite an impression on Mrs Thatcher. She had been keeping an eye on Gorbachev for some time, thinking that he would be a good Soviet leader. What she knew of him seemed 'modestly encouraging'. 'He was clearly the best-educated member of the Politburo,' she writes, 'not that anybody would have described this group of elderly soldiers and bureaucrats as intellectuals.' However, relations with the Soviets were still far from healthy – in fact, direct communication with them was all but impossible.

In February 1984, she had attended the funeral of the Soviet leader Yuri Andropov, whose death elevated Gorbachev to his being the second most powerful man in the USSR behind Konstantin U. Chernenko.

Now, the man who would become Soviet leader was at Chequers. Once the small talk had ended, Gorbachev began telling Mrs Thatcher about the Soviets' economic programmes. He spoke of ambitious irrigation schemes and the way industrial capacity was adapted to avoid unemployment. Once again, her detestation of collectivism came to the fore, as she asked whether there might be reform on a free-enterprise basis, with incentives for entrepreneurs. She clearly did not like the idea that everything should be state-run, though Gorbachev was proud of what he saw as the superiority of the Soviet system: there were higher growth rates and the Soviet people were happy. Challenging this assertion, she asked him why, if this were so, the authorities there did not allow people to leave the country as easily as they could leave Britain. She was also critical of the restrictions on Jewish emigration to Israel.

Gorbachev was highly suspicious of Ronald Reagan's Strategic Defense Initiative (SDI, the so-called 'Star Wars'), and Mrs Thatcher was wary that Gorbachev might try to drive a wedge between Britain and the USA. She was quick to assure him, however, that there would be no question of his dividing them.

She liked Gorbachev's style. For one thing, she says, he smiled, he laughed, he used his hands for emphasis, he modulated his voice and was a good debater. In *The Downing Street Years* she recalled that:

'If at this stage I had paid attention only to the

content of Mr Gorbachev's remarks – largely the standard Marxist line – I would have to conclude that he was cast in the usual communist mould. But his personality could not have been more different from the wooden ventriloquism of the average Soviet apparatchik. *

A degree of resentment

In January 1985 Margaret Thatcher achieved a rare distinction in the world of academia: she did *not* receive an honorary degree from her alma mater. More than a thousand dons assembled at Oxford's splendid Sheldonian Theatre, filling the floor space and the galleries, to vote on a proposal to confer upon Mrs Thatcher the honorary degree of Doctor of Civil Law. After a two-hour debate, the result was finally announced that there would be no honorary degree for Mrs Margaret Hilda Thatcher.

I went to Oxford University, but I've never let that hold me back.

What made this so unusual was that, since 1946, every prime minister educated at Oxford had received an honorary degree. Another rarity was the sheer number of dons who attended. On previous occasions, nothing approaching this large gathering had been witnessed for this type of occasion.

There were also indignant outbursts from those assembled, who were more than a little miffed by her education policies. Mrs Thatcher enacted revenge of sorts in 1999, when she accepted an honour from Oxford's rival, Cambridge, who asked her to become a companion of the elite Guild of Cambridge Benefactors. The offer came after her fundraising efforts for Cambridge during lecture tours in the USA.

A year of summits

In March that year, Mrs Thatcher was in Moscow for the funeral of the Soviet leader Konstantin Chernenko, and again met Mikhail Gorbachev. On Chernenko's death, Gorbachev ('Gorby', as he was nicknamed in the West) became General Secretary of the Communist Party and, as such, the Soviet leader. Later in 1988 he would also assume the presidency of the USSR after the retirement of Andrei Gromyko.

After the visit to Moscow, Mrs Thatcher set off on a ten-day tour of the Far East. Summits were once again dotted through the Prime Minister's busy year: the Bonn G7 summit, the Anglo-German summit at Chequers, the Brussels EC summit – and they were just May's engagements.

In September, Mrs Thatcher carried out a wide-ranging government reshuffle, with Norman Tebbit becoming party Chairman and Kenneth Clarke, John MacGregor and Kenneth Baker joining the Cabinet.

This was also the month that saw twenty-four Soviet diplomats expelled from Britain on alleged spying charges. It was an expulsion that Mrs Thatcher herself authorized.

Heseltine storms out

November 1988 saw Mrs Thatcher chairing a meeting of ministers to consider entry into the European Exchange Rate Mechanism (ERM). She firmly vetoed the idea, beginning to consolidate her reputation as a Euro-sceptic. She saw no good reason to allow British monetary policy to be decided by the Bundesbank rather than the Treasury, and did not think the industrial lobby currently pressing to join the ERM would continue to be so enthusiastic once they saw that it would make their goods uncompetitive.

Has he resigned or has he gone for a pee?
TO CABINET COLLEAGUES ON MICHAEL HESELTINE'S RESIGNATION

The incident that generated the most media coverage during that period, was when Tarzan himself (the sobriquet of the then Defence Secretary Michael Heseltine, accorded him because of his big flowing hairdo) walked out of a Cabinet meeting over what came to be known as 'the Westland affair'. The Westland helicopter company, based in Yeovil in Somerset, was in deep financial trouble. There were media reports of rifts between Heseltine and the Trade Secretary, Leon Brittan, over the future of the company and what the government could do. Westland was Britain's only helicopter manufacturer and relied heavily on government contracts. Heseltine had said as far back as April 1985 that, if Westland were looking for lucrative orders from the MoD, they would look in vain.

Bidding to take over Westland was one Alan Bristow, and he had threatened to withdraw the bid unless there were government assurances of orders. Meetings had been held between Heseltine, Brittan, Chancellor Nigel Lawson and Mrs Thatcher, among others. Heseltine had suggested a scheme to provide £30 million in aid. What they did agree on was that Westland should not be allowed to go into receivership, which it would if Bristow withdrew his bid. Rather than provide aid to the firm during the takeover bid – which would have been illegal, anyway – the Bank of England should be encouraged to bring together the main creditors, so that new management could be put in place and a new strategy for recovery developed.

Bristow did withdraw his bid, but then a large privately owned US company, Sikorsky, made it known that it wanted to make a bid. Westland's new management were not in favour, and Tebbit and Heseltine were against it, too. The latter thought a European buyer should be sought.

Eventually, Sikorsky made an offer for a substantial stake in Westland, and the company's board said it would accept this – but Heseltine was still dead against it. The three European companies being considered did not seem to be shaping up as serious actors in this heightening drama. However, Westland had been collaborating with Sikorsky for decades, which Mrs Thatcher and her supporters in this argument saw as a distinct advantage.

The row reached a climax in January 1986, when Heseltine famously walked out of a Cabinet meeting and resigned his post over the affair. His Defence post was given to George Younger.

Mrs Thatcher says in her memoir that she has learned since that other colleagues at that Cabinet meeting were stunned by Heseltine's decision to walk out. She, however, was not. Heseltine had made his decision, and that was that. Of Heseltine, she writes:

❦Michael and I are similar in some ways, very different in others. We are ambitious, single-minded and believe in efficiency and results. But whereas with me it is certain political principles that provide a reference point and inner strength, for Michael such things are unnecessary. His own overwhelming belief in himself is sufficient.❧

She was under no illusions that there would be a huge furore over the matter, but, for her, it was the proverbial storm in a teacup. It was a crisis that had been created from a small issue by what she describes as 'a giant ego'.

She maintains that at the time she did not know whether Heseltine had come to that Cabinet meeting having already determined on his subsequent and dramatic course of action. However, she does believe that he came to the meeting very well prepared.

Leon Brittan himself was to resign over the same issue after further complications over correspondence concerning the then Chief Executive of British Aerospace, Sir Raymond Lygo. It had been suggested that Brittan had had a meeting with Lygo and that Brittan had suggested that British Aerospace's involvement in a European consortium of companies was against the national interest. However, the letter in question was marked private and confidential, and Brittan felt obliged to keep it that way, leading to accusations that he had misled the House of Commons.

It was clearly a complex issue that did not turn out to be as easily resolved as Margaret Thatcher had at first ancipated. In the event, that affair was another very embarrassing and undermining episode in the eleven-and-a-half-year history of the Thatcher government.

TAXING TIMES:

Margaret Defends the Indefensible

' I was asked whether I was trying to restore
Victorian values. I said straight out I was.
And I am. '

The miners' strike and the Westland affair had tested the
Thatcher government sorely during the 1983–7 period. A
further embarrassment had come knocking in April 1986,
when America flew a bombing mission on Libya in
retaliation for terrorist attacks on Americans elsewhere,
and most of the aircraft had been allowed – by Mrs
Thatcher – to fly from British air bases. This may have
bolstered the US–UK 'special relationship', but it did not go
down well with many people in Britain.

Fortunately for Mrs Thatcher, any fallout from these
difficulties was soon being replaced by the mutual slapping
of backs during a period of economic boom, with the newly
privatized industries pouring money into the government
coffers and the British people being encouraged to become
part of the share-owning elite. Many had been able to buy
shares in British Gas and British Telecom, and Mrs
Thatcher and her ministers clearly thought – or wanted the
public to think – that this would give them a real say in the
way their utilities were to be run.

During March and April of 1987, Mrs Thatcher made a

historic visit to Moscow, and, after numerous photo opportunities, she was perceived as a new bridge between West and East. Things seemed good, and the time was ripe to call a general election, which she did: for 11 June 1987.

Clothes maketh the woman

During the election campaign, Mrs Thatcher became even more concerned about her image – notably her sartorial appearance. Gordon Reece continued to be on hand to advise as she began to take a closer interest in the clothes she wore. She felt that the impression that she was to make during the election campaign was vital. There would be personal appearances, speeches, meetings, television appearances. While she was in opposition she had worn clothes from various suppliers, but, since she had become Prime Minister, her sartorial considerations, she felt, were now more important than ever. And so it was that she commissioned from Aquascutum some suits, jackets and shirts – what she called 'working clothes' – to be used during the election campaign.

> We got a really good consensus during the last election. Consensus behind my convictions.

Her clothing was to become even more important when televising of the proceedings inside the House of Commons was introduced in November 1989. She realized, too, that stripes and checks, while looking attractive in the flesh, could dazzle television viewers because of the way certain patterns are treated in the transmission process. She was also aware of the possibility – horror of horrors! – of wearing the same outfit on successive occasions. Definitely not the done thing. So she had a record kept of which outfit she wore at each Prime Minister's Questions session so that this stylistic sin should not be committed, because, when she had worn the same suit twice on the trot, people had commented on it and journalists had written about it.

We can only speculate on whether Margaret Thatcher's choice of clothing made a contribution to the subsequent election success, but, when the Tories won the 1987 ballot, they did so with a majority of 102 seats. They won 376 seats, with 42.3 per cent of the vote, to Labour's 229 seats, with 30.8 per cent.

Her government immediately set about drawing up plans for its third term of office – plans to reform the education system; plans for a new 'community charge', more popularly known as the poll tax, which would help lead to the Tories' eventual downfall; and plans to separate the purchasers from the providers within the NHS, introducing competition – and a good deal of confusion and ill will – into the health system.

The Bruges speech

In July, the Single European Act came into being. Agreed in

1985, this had now been approved by all twelve (as the number then was) member states. As well as introducing a weighted-majority system as a means of speeding up the journey to a single market, the Single European Act gave formal status to the European Council, which had provided much of the impetus for a single European market. The European Parliament was also given greater status and authority, and there was agreement on certain common policies on matters such as the environment, taxes and health.

> ‘ We have not successfully rolled back the
> frontiers of the state in Britain only to see
> them reimposed at a European level, with a
> European super-state exercising a new
> dominance from Brussels. ’

Problems began to beset the Thatcher administration at this time. The boom of the late 1980s led to an overheating of the economy, resulting in the doubling of interest rates in 1988. Meanwhile, there was disharmony over the whole question of Europe, with Mrs Thatcher often opposing the Foreign Secretary, Sir Geoffrey Howe, on matters of European integration. Some point to Mrs Thatcher's notable 'Bruges speech' of September 1988 as being the moment at which Britain's Tories turned from being relatively pro-European to being Euro-sceptics.

Mrs Thatcher had acquiesced to Foreign Office wishes

that she accept the invitation to speak, and she began by pointing out how much Britain had contributed – and continued to contribute – to Europe. She went on to argue, however, that Britain should not look only to Western Europe, but also to those countries in the East. The West had something to learn from them, she insisted, in spite of what she saw as their dreadful experiences. Indeed, it was the experiences of Soviet countries that she used to make a salient point:

> ❛It is ironic that just when those countries such as the Soviet Union, which have tried to run everything from the centre, are learning that success depends on dispersing power and decisions away from the centre, some in the [European] Community seem to want to move in the opposite direction.❜

It was important, she told her audience, to have a European Single Market with the minimum of regulation; Europe must not be protectionist; NATO was important and anything that might result in a Western European alternative to it must be resisted.

The speech brought strong reactions – stronger reactions than Thatcher expected. Pro-Europeans were horrified. Even that evening, she had a verbal set-to with the Belgian leader Wilfried Martens and his Deputy Prime Minister and Foreign Minister. 'But perhaps that was only to be expected from a small country which thought it could wield more power inside a federal Europe than outside it,' she records in *The Downing Street Years.*

> ❝ Let Europe be a family of nations, understanding each other better, appreciating each other more, doing more together, but relishing our national identity no less than our common European endeavour. Let us have a Europe which plays its full part in the wider world, which looks outward, not inward, and which preserves that Atlantic Community – that Europe on both sides of the Atlantic – which is our noblest inheritance and our greatest strength. ❞

A hateful law

The Tories were traditionally known for taking a dim view of homosexuality. By the 1980s a gay lifestyle had become increasingly acceptable in society, but not among the party faithful. They particularly didn't like the fact that teachers and local authorities wanted to recognize that gay people had a right to exist and to express their love according to their nature. A rash of tabloid articles claiming that left-wing councils were wasting huge amounts of taxpayers' money on gay and lesbian groups emboldened the Conservatives to act.

> ❝ Children who need to be taught to respect traditional moral values are being taught that they have an inalienable right to be gay. ❞

While Section 28 (formerly Clause 28) was a clause added to the Local Government Act 1988 by Dame Jill Knight, it was clearly evidence of the Thatcher government's wish to stop what it chose to view as some kind of agenda to 'promote' homosexuality. What many found especially objectionable, in what was the first piece of specifically anti-gay legislation to be introduced since Victorian times, was the wording. After stating that no local authority should 'intentionally promote homosexuality or publish material with the intention of promoting homosexuality', it went on to say that local authorities should not 'promote the teaching in any maintained school of the acceptability of homosexuality as a pretended family relationship'.

Not only was the legislation a huge affront to Britain's gay community, it proved a rallying point for human-rights campaigners. Nevertheless, it has endured: so far New Labour has failed to have the law taken off the statute book, although it has tried half-heartedly (and north of the border the Labour-controlled Scottish Parliament succeeded in 2000).

In May 2000, the journalist Nick Cohen wrote in the *Observer*, 'Clause 28 is Thatcherite gesture politics. Apart from giving nail-bombers and queer-bashers a complicit wink of encouragement, it has achieved nothing because there are no miscreants to punish.' The reference to nail-bombers was to the fatal explosion that had occurred in Old Compton Street, Soho, outside a gay pub called the Admiral Duncan.

Also in 2000, Ivan Massow – a gay businessman who had been Baroness Thatcher's official companion at the 1999 Tory Party conference – described her as 'completely doolally, a bonkers old bird who says the wrong thing at every possible moment' in a *Guardian* interview dated 26 October. He was referring to his failed attempt the previous year to gain her support for the repeal of Section 28.

Farewell, Ron

On the other side of the Atlantic, the USA elected a new president, in the shape of George Bush (now, of course, known as George Bush, Sr) in November 1987. In the middle of that month Margaret Thatcher flew to Washington, DC, for a three-day farewell visit with Ronald Reagan.

Mrs Thatcher says that she 'breathed a sigh of relief' when Bush defeated his Democrat opponent Michael Dukakis to become the first incumbent Vice-President since 1836 to be elected President. It 'ensured continuity' as she put it, and moreover, continuity of the kind that suited her. She was later aggrieved to discover, however, that the new team in the White House saw Germany as its main European partner in leadership. In her memoirs, she records that this attitude of the Bush administration 'encouraged the integration of Europe without seeming to understand fully what it meant and which sometimes seemed to underestimate the need for a strong nuclear defence'. She could not, therefore, rely on American co-operation, as before. This was important, because, with the arrival of 1989, the Eastern European communist system was beginning to break up.

Another unpopular measure

The end of the Thatcher era was marked by one of the most unpopular pieces of legislation any government has introduced: the community charge, widely dubbed 'the poll tax'. Its introduction, and Mrs Thatcher's defence of it in the face of overwhelming opposition, played a vital role in discrediting her as leader of the Tory Party. A member of HM Government would not be heard of speaking of 'the poll tax' on TV or radio, of course: it was 'the community charge'. But to everyone else it was the poll tax, and it was widely loathed.

> We introduced the community charge. I still like to call it that. I like the Poles – I never had any intention of taxing them.

Poll tax is not a new concept. The ancient Greeks and Romans levied such a tax on vanquished peoples. After the American Civil War, a poll tax was introduced by the southern states in order to prevent former slaves from having the vote. If they couldn't afford to pay the tax, they didn't have the right to vote. In Britain – or, more accurately, in England – a poll tax was introduced as early as 1377. It was reimposed at intervals until 1698, and was often an important means of raising revenue for wars.

Margaret Thatcher's poll tax was first introduced in Scotland in 1989 and in the rest of the country a year later.

If the government thought that this testing of the water north of the border would prepare those elsewhere for this new way of collecting local taxes, they were wrong.

A number of Labour MPs had indicated since 1988 that they were prepared to break the law and refuse to pay. This civil disobedience was not confined merely to MPs: in Trafalgar Square, the night before the poll tax was to be introduced in England and Wales, there was a demonstration that led to rioting. Mrs Thatcher attributes the disturbances to 'a group of troublemakers':

> Scaffolding on a building site in the square was dismantled and used as missiles; fires were started and cars destroyed. Almost 400 policemen were injured and 339 people were arrested. It was a mercy that no one was killed. I was appalled at such wickedness.

Her attempt to bulldoze her way through public opinion by first introducing the tax, and then by standing by it in the face of mass opposition from the country, and even from many of those in her own party, cost her dearly, both financially and politically. While her supporters had often pointed to her ability to stand firm in the face of adversity as one of her most admirable traits, in this instance, her obstinacy did her little good. She still maintains that it was the size of the bills being sent out that was the problem. The demonstrations and non-payments of the tax did not undermine her determination to continue with the poll tax, only to try to ensure that the burden was not too high on the 'conscientious middle'.

❝ Given time, it would have been seen as one of the most far-reaching and beneficial reforms ever made in the working of local government. ❞
ON THE COMMUNITY CHARGE

On the same day as demonstrators made their way to Whitehall Mrs Thatcher was addressing her party's central council in Cheltenham, where she attacked local authorities for spending too much. 'Many of the bills for the community charge which people are now receiving are far too high,' she said. 'I share the outrage they feel. But let's be clear: it's not the way the money is raised, it's the amount of money that local government is spending. That's the real problem. No scheme, no matter how ingenious, could pay for high spending with low charges.'

It was only after Mrs Thatcher's premiership had ended and John Major had taken over that the Tories eventually dumped the poll tax. It was replaced in 1991 by a local charge that was only partly based on property value and is known as the council tax. The 'community charge' had produced a bruising time for the Tories.

The IRA claims another victim

Throughout this difficult time, the rest of political life had continued apace. The Prime Minister began a six-day visit to Africa at the end of March 1989, and Mikhail Gorbachev visited Britain for three days in April. In July, Mrs Thatcher reshuffled her Cabinet, and among the beneficiaries of that was John Major who was moved to the Foreign and Commonwealth Office. Nigel Lawson resigned during the subsequent fallout from the Westland affair, and Major's career took another step forward when he succeeded Lawson as Chancellor of the Exchequer.

A threat to Mrs Thatcher's leadership – although one she clearly did not deign to take too seriously – came towards the end of the year, when Sir Anthony Meyer stood against her. He announced his decision on 28 November, and Mrs Thatcher beat him in the battle for the leadership on 5 December. There had been talk of her being challenged, possibly by a stalking-horse for the real contender, Michael Heseltine, but Meyer decided for reasons of his own to challenge his leader. The result: Margaret Thatcher, 314 votes; Anthony Meyer, 33; there were twenty-four spoiled papers and three abstentions. Despite the decisive outcome of the ballot, Mrs Thatcher was advised that the contest had revealed some discontent among the Tory Party with the status quo.

July 1990 would once again see the IRA murder one of Mrs Thatcher's political allies. A year before, the IRA had killed ten bandsmen at the Royal Marines School of Music at Deal in Kent. In 1990, bombs went off outside the home of the party treasurer Alistair McAlpine and outside the party's Carlton Club. The following month, Mrs Thatcher experienced once again something of what she had felt back in 1979 when Airey Neave had been killed by an IRA assassin's bomb, and when she had heard back in 1984 of the deaths in the Brighton hotel bombing.

The IRA had singled out Ian Gow, the MP for Eastbourne and a former parliamentary private secretary under Mrs Thatcher. He held no government office, but was known to be a staunch Unionist when it came to Northern Ireland politics. As such, he was the enemy of the IRA. It was a Monday, 30 July. Gow started his car in the drive of his house during what should have been a routine day, and was blown up. Distraught by the news, Margaret Thatcher also shuddered at the memory that her daughter Carol had travelled with Gow the previous weekend in the same car when they had gone to take the Gows' dog for a walk.

The subsequent by-election – in October – saw Gow's old seat go to the Liberals with a swing of 20 per cent. The opinion polls were not looking rosy for the Tories: Labour had taken a substantial lead.

Then there was the question of Sir Geoffrey Howe, Mrs Thatcher's trusted ally with whom she was now at loggerheads. On *Weekend World*, the Brian Walden programme that had been one of Mrs Thatcher's first television platforms, Howe set in motion the Prime Minister's political downfall.

END OF AN INNINGS:
Margaret Makes a Tearful Exit

> ❝ Margaret Thatcher was beyond argument a great Prime Minister. Her tragedy is that she may be remembered less for the brilliance of her many achievements than for the recklessness with which she later sought to impose her increasingly uncompromising views. ❞
>
> GEOFFREY HOWE, 1994

Richard Edward Geoffrey Howe sat as MP for Surrey East, having served as the member for both Bebington and Reigate. He had served as Solicitor General under Edward Heath, when he had gained a knighthood. Since the Tories' return to power under Margaret Thatcher in 1979, he had been Chancellor of the Exchequer and Foreign Secretary. Though he and Mrs Thatcher had previously enjoyed a very good relationship, her handling of the Cabinet reshuffle of 1989 first sowed seeds of discontent between them, when she at first retracted, then again offered him the post of Deputy Prime Minister. It was also thought that he was unhappy at being taken away from the Foreign Office. It was over Europe, however, that their differences came to a head.

On 27 September 1990 Margaret Thatcher arrived in

Rome to attend a summit. That week Geoffrey Howe was in a television studio, telling Brian Walden that the party did not, in fact, oppose the principle of a single currency. The implication was that he believed that Mrs Thatcher might be won round to that opinion. As soon as she returned she was questioned about Howe's comments at the first possible opportunity.

In response to a barrage of questions she stressed that 'a single currency is not the policy of this government'. There was a qualification to this: it was that the Conservatives' own proposal for a parallel or 'common' currency in the form of a 'hard ecu' could evolve towards a single currency. (The ecu, or European currency unit, was a common unit of exchange in the European Union, introduced in 1979 as part of the ERM.) It was a question of interpretations. She thought this hypothetical qualification about the hard ecu could have been used by Howe to keep the possibility of an eventual single currency on the agenda – but this was not the government's intention, and Thatcher felt there had been a basic dishonesty in Howe's interpretation. She said that, in her view, the hard ecu would not become widely used throughout the European Community, except by commerce. Ordinary people would prefer to keep their own currency.

❛ Europe is strongest when it grows through willing co-operation and practical measures, not compulsion or bureaucratic dreams. ❜

She was emphatic: 'This government believes in the pound sterling,' she said unequivocally. In *The Downing Street Years*, Lady Thatcher says that this wrangle set Howe on the road to resignation, although to her, and maybe to him, it is still unclear exactly why. She did not even know, she says, whether he really wanted a single currency, and had not said exactly where he stood, only where she should not stand. She felt that the rift between her and Geoffrey Howe was now as much a matter of personal antipathy as of differences in policy.

That week, in a Cabinet meeting, Mrs Thatcher took Howe to task – probably, she feels, too sharply – about the preparation of the legislative programme. The same afternoon, Howe asked to see her urgently and announced that he intended to resign. She asked if he would put off his decision till the following morning. He said he had already cancelled a speech he was due to give that evening at the Royal Overseas League, and that news of his intentions was bound to get out to the wider world. And so his resignation was announced.

Mrs Thatcher said that his departure was a huge relief for her: by this time they were finding each other's company almost intolerable. Many found it surprising that he had remained so long in a position that he clearly disliked and resented.

She was in no doubt that Howe's departure would wreak political havoc. Again there was talk of a leadership bid, no doubt involving Michael Heseltine. Her relationship with Howe had soured to the extent that she did not expect for one moment that Howe would

THE WORLD ACCORDING TO MARGARET THATCHER

remain silent about his reasons for resignation.

She reshuffled the Cabinet yet again. She was keen to bring Norman Tebbit back into government, but he needed to look after his wife, who had been injured in the Brighton bombing six years before. She spent Saturday, 3 November, at Chequers, working on a speech, and her press secretary, Bernard Ingham, rang her that evening to read an open letter that Heseltine had written to his constituency in Cheltenham, talking about the need for the government to chart a new course on Europe. It was the first step in Heseltine's bid for the leadership.

Of course, the papers the following day – 4 November – were full of stories about a possible leadership challenge. They contained opinion-poll findings, too, which looked very bad, with Labour in one of them shown to be 21 per cent ahead.

It was still not certain that Heseltine would choose to stand for the leadership, but Mrs Thatcher and her advisers decided that the continuing speculation was doing the party and the government no good at all, and it would be best for all to try to get the leadership campaign out of the way as quickly as possible.

On 12 November – a Monday – Mrs Thatcher delivered a speech at the Lord Mayor's Banquet in the Guildhall. In it, she used a cricketing metaphor to describe her currently beleaguered status and her determination to emerge triumphant from the crisis:

> ‘I am still at the crease, though the bowling has been pretty hostile of late, and, in case anyone doubted it,

can I assure you there will be no ducking of bouncers, no stonewalling, no playing for time. The bowling's going to get hit all round the ground.'

The reference to the quintessentially English game of cricket would rebound like a well-placed fast ball rising from the crease to meet the bat – or, in her case, the stumps – when Geoffrey Howe spoke in the Commons the next day about his decision to resign. Margaret Thatcher decided that she would stay on after questions in order to listen to him. It was a powerful performance, she records – 'the most powerful of his career'. She says that, if the speech failed in its apparent purpose of explaining policy differences between him and her, it succeeded in what she saw as its real purpose, which was to damage her. She describes it in her memoirs as 'cool, forensic, light at points, and poisonous'.

In his speech, Howe famously met her cricketing metaphor of the previous evening with his own. He claimed that her earlier remarks about the hard ecu had undermined both the Chancellor of the Exchequer and the Governor of the Bank of England.

'It is rather like sending your opening batsmen to the crease, only for them to find, at the moment the first balls are bowled, that their bats have been broken before the game by the team captain.'

His final line proved to be particularly devastating, for he declared that the time had come 'for others to consider their own responses to the tragic conflict of loyalty with which I have myself wrestled for perhaps too long.'

As Mrs Thatcher sat and listened to the speech her mask of composure hid turbulent emotions. She already knew this would be taken as an open invitation for Michael Heseltine to challenge her for the leadership. She felt bitterly betrayed by her former friend and ally. Geoffrey Howe, she said, would be remembered from this point on not for his work as a government minister but for 'this final act of bile and treachery'.

Campaign dinner at Chequers

On 14 November, Mrs Thatcher received official notification that Heseltine would indeed stand for the leadership. It did not come as a surprise to her and there was never any question that she would not fight. Her own nomination was proposed by Douglas Hurd and seconded by the man who would eventually take over from her as party leader and Prime Minister, John Major. This, she says, was intended to demonstrate the Cabinet's support for her.

She immediately set about a campaign of press interviews. It was not long before Heseltine's campaign, too, was in full swing. Perhaps deliberately, he declared his intentions to challenge some of her most controversial policies, promising a review of the hated poll tax and talking of a transfer of the costs of services such as education to central taxation. Margaret Thatcher had already dismissed such a transfer out of hand, warning in the House of Commons that it might mean either large cuts in other public-spending areas or a five-pence rise in income tax. In response to his sallies she pressed home an attack on his approach in a *Times* interview, criticizing his long-standing corporatist and interventionist views.

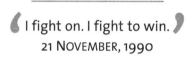

I fight on. I fight to win.
21 NOVEMBER, 1990

On the Saturday evening, 17 November, the Thatchers invited several of the key players to dinner at Chequers, and they made an assessment of the situation. The figures for support seemed quite favourable to her at this point, even allowing for the 'lie factor'. She felt far from secure, however, recalling that Ted Heath had himself remarked that such figures were not to be trusted, and that some people were on the books of both sides.

The following day, Sunday, 18 November, Mrs Thatcher departed for the Conference on Security and Cooperation in Europe (CSCE) summit in Paris, the social climax of which was to be a ballet performance at the Palace of Versailles. Presidents Bush and Gorbachev were also at the summit. During the time she was in France, her staff kept a line open to London. In spite of the turmoil that must have been churning her emotions, she put a brave face on things and turned to the work at hand.

News eventually came through to Paris that, in the first

ballot, she had received 204 votes in the ballot; Michael Heseltine had received 152; there were 16 abstentions. This was not good. Although she had beaten Heseltine and achieved a clear majority of the parliamentary party (more votes in defeat that John Major would win when he himself won the leadership), she had not won by a large enough margin to avoid a second ballot.

> The Labour party is led by a pygmy and we are led by a giant. We have decided that the answer to our problems is to find a pygmy of our own.
> CECIL PARKINSON, 1990

There ensued a flurry of telephone calls from her supporters. Douglas Hurd urged her to stand in a second ballot, pledging her his support; and she knew she would receive support from John Major. She went down to meet the press gathered outside Number 10 and greeted them breezily:

> I am naturally very pleased that I got more than half the parliamentary party and disappointed that it is not quite enough to win on the first ballot, so I confirm it is my intention to let my name go forward for the second ballot.

Douglas Hurd then addressed the assembled

journalists: 'I would just like to make a brief comment on the ballot result. The Prime Minister continues to have my full support, and I am sorry that this destructive, unnecessary contest should be prolonged in this way.'

She was due at the Palace of Versailles to see the ballet, but had to telephone her hosts to say she would be late, adding that the proceedings should begin without her. As it turned out, when she arrived at the palace, where President Mitterrand was waiting for her, he said, 'Of course, we would never have started without you.'

Mrs Thatcher arrived back in Britain just before midday on Wednesday, 21 November. It had been agreed that she should see members of the Cabinet one by one. The staff at Number 10 applauded and cheered as she arrived, and from one supporter a thousand red roses had arrived. As the day wore on, more and more flowers were delivered to Number 10, bathing every corridor and staircase in a riot of vibrant colour.

Denis Thatcher advised his wife not to stand, but to withdraw her name. However, while she was not sure that it was a battle she could win, she was determined to fight on. She was convinced that it was extremely important to stop Michael Heseltine at all costs. She consulted other members of her camp and the assessment was that it was difficult to know how her support stood with MPs, although many would undoubtedly fight hard for her. The biggest weakness, she felt, was among her own Cabinet ministers.

The discussion among the Thatcher camp held that, because the Whips' Office had received many messages from backbenchers and ministers saying that she should withdraw, a candidate would be required who could beat Michael Heseltine – and they doubted that Margaret Thatcher now could. However, whom else could they turn to? Although she admired him and was grateful for his continued loyalty, Mrs Thatcher did not believe that Douglas Hurd could beat Heseltine. She therefore looked to John Major as her possible successor. If she were to withdraw, would he be able to win? She thought his prospects at best uncertain.

There was also a fear that she would be humiliated in a second ballot and, even if she won by a small majority, the job of uniting the party would be very difficult indeed because of the perceived loss of authority. There was much talk of the poll tax. Most people were worried about this, not about Europe, and the Thatcher camp were hoping that something could be done. In spite of Mrs Thatcher's unbending adherence to this hated piece of legislation, it was obvious that it was coming back to haunt her. Clearly, Michael Heseltine's promise to take action on the poll tax was becoming attractive to MPs, particularly to those in the north-west of England where resistance to it was especially virulent. Ironically, it was those MPs and ministers who felt she could not win a second ballot who were her strongest supporters – people such as Norman Lamont, John Gummer, Michael Howard and Peter Lilley.

And so the thoughts that were going through Mrs Thatcher's mind as she agonized over whether to allow her name to be put forward for the second ballot were: (a) even her strongest supporters doubted that she could win; (b) there was a belief that even if she succeeded she would not be able to unite the party in preparation for a subsequent general election; and (c) there was the spectre of humiliation if she were to fight and lose.

All of this was being discussed at a meeting with other members of her camp. She told them she would reflect on what had been discussed, and she was to recall years later that her resolve at meetings such as this one had been weakened. As she left for the House of Commons that evening, to give a statement on her Paris summit, she called to assembled journalists in Downing Street, saying, 'I fight on. I fight to win!' However, she recalls that she was interested to see on television news later that she looked more confident than she felt.

That evening, she asked Douglas Hurd to nominate her for the second ballot, which he agreed to do. She telephoned John Major and told him that she had decided to stand again. She asked if he would second Hurd's nomination. Before he replied, there was an almost palpable hesitation, a moment's silence on the phone line. However, he did agree to second her. Later, when she referred to this, she would lie that there had been no hesitation. But she recalls in her memoirs that both of them knew otherwise.

We now know from John Major's own memoirs of 1999 that he secretly drew up plans to stand for the leadership while he was publicly voicing his support for Mrs Thatcher. Moments after he had signed her nomination paper for the second ballot, he had asked his wife, Norma, to type out a letter putting forward his name for the leadership. It was a cloak-and-dagger operation in which Major gave two sets of documents, both in sealed envelopes, to a chauffeur, to take them to London. His letter was to be kept secret if Mrs Thatcher won the battle and stayed on.

> ❛ [John Major] has the makings of a great prime minister, which I'm sure he will be in a very short time ❜

Mrs Thatcher's next call was at Buckingham Palace, where she sought an audience with the Queen and informed her that she would be standing in the second ballot. She then saw her Cabinet ministers one by one. While each told her she had his backing, each also said he did not think she could win. Furthermore, it was generally thought that Douglas Hurd and John Major – who had, respectively, proposed and seconded her – should now be released from their obligation, and themselves be allowed to stand, because both had a better chance than she did. Without the support of the Cabinet, Mrs Thatcher knew she was fighting a losing battle. There was a suggestion that she should carry on in the short-term, but only on the understanding that she was to stand down immediately after Christmas if she won. The idea was that she would be able to see through the Gulf crisis, which had begun with Saddam Hussein's annexing of Kuwait that August. She could not accept such a deal, however, because it meant she would have no authority in the shortterm.

After she had summoned and seen all her sad captains, she dictated a statement to be read at the cabinet meeting the following day, but she would return to Number 10 to talk to her husband Denis before taking a final decision.

At this point, Norman Tebbit arrived in her study with Michael Portillo, who was Minister of State at the Department of the Environment and responsible for the discredited poll tax. Portillo was a passionate supporter, says Mrs Thatcher, of everything she stood for. He tried to convince her that Cabinet members were misinterpreting the situation and that, with an effective campaign, it would still be possible to reverse this downward slide.

After more encouraging words from other MPs, Mrs Thatcher did return to Number 10 and went to see Denis, who gave her his comfort. Before retiring to bed, she reflected that it was now going to be important to ensure that John Major's own nomination paper should be ready (she did not, of course, know that he had himself ensured its readiness) to be submitted before the tight deadline if, indeed, she decided not to enter the second ballot. She had still not quite made up her mind.

At 7.30 the next morning – Thursday, 22 November – she made it known that she had finally resolved to resign, and plans were made for an audience with the Queen. She went into the Cabinet Room and made a statement to those who were there:

'Having consulted widely among my colleagues, I

have concluded that the unity of the party and the prospects of victory in a general election would be better served if I stood down to enable Cabinet colleagues to enter the ballot for the leadership. I should like to thank all those in the Cabinet and outside who have given me such dedicated support. "

The Cabinet meeting then resumed and conducted its scheduled business, which must have seemed mundane indeed to the woman who had served as Prime Minister for eleven and a half years, and who had now just tendered her resignation.

Bowing out

Things happen quickly when a leader is suddenly removed from office. After she had seen the Queen to tell her of her decision, Mrs Thatcher returned to Number 10 for lunch, had a drink with members of her staff, and noticed that preparations of a decidedly valedictory nature were happening around her: things were being collected together and packed; outstanding constituency business was being looked at; Denis Thatcher was clearing his own desk.

" It was treachery with a smile on its face. Perhaps that was the worst thing of all. "
DESCRIBING HER TREATMENT BY THE CABINET IN 1990

'I'm enjoying this'

That afternoon, Mrs Thatcher had to respond to a no-confidence debate initiated by Labour, in which Neil Kinnock rose to attack her for the last time in her role as his opposite number. She used the occasion to restate her conviction that her government's record had been a spotless one. She said that, ten years before, the eastern part of Europe had lain under totalitarian rule, and its people knew neither rights nor liberties. However, today, we lived in a Europe in which democracy and human rights were spreading widely, and where the threat to our security from the overwhelming conventional forces of the Warsaw Pact had been removed. The Berlin Wall had been torn down. The Cold War was now at an end.

> These immense changes did not come about by chance. They have been achieved by strength and resolution in defence, and by a refusal ever to be intimidated. No one in Eastern Europe believes that their countries would be free had it not been for those Western governments who were prepared to defend liberty and who kept alive their hope that one day Eastern Europe, too, would enjoy freedom.

In chiding Kinnock for his party's decision to bring a

no-confidence motion, Mrs Thatcher had her last swipe – as Prime Minister at least – at the unions:

⁶The opposition's real reason [for the motion] is the leadership election for the Conservative Party, which is a democratic election according to rules which have been public knowledge for many years – one member, one vote. That is a far cry from the way in which the Labour Party does these things. Two in every five votes for its leader are cast by the trade union block votes, which have a bigger say than Labour members in that decision: precious little democracy there.⁹

The Tories had curbed 'the monopoly power of trade unions to control, even to victimize' individual workers, she said. 'Labour would return us to conflict, confrontation and government by the consent of the TUC.'

She fended off questions from opposition MPs about the level of unemployment, the gap between rich and poor, inflation. Hers was a bravura performance by any standards and at no point was she stuck for an answer.

After a question concerning the prospect of a single European currency and an independent central bank, her old sparring partner Dennis Skinner, the brusque, no-nonsense MP for Bolsover, had joked that she would be its governor. What a good idea, she said. But, if she were, there would be no central European bank. The single currency was about politics, she said, about a federal

Europe by the back door:

‘So I shall consider the proposal of the honourable member for Bolsover. Now where were we? I'm enjoying this.’

She ended by speaking of the incipient Gulf War:

‘There is something else which one feels. That is a sense of this country's destiny: the centuries of history and experience which ensure that, when principles have to be defended, when good has to be upheld and when evil has to be overcome, Britain will take up arms. It is because we on this side [of the house] have never flinched from difficult decisions that this house and this country can have confidence in this government today.’

She sat down to raucous cheers.

Having made her last speech as Prime Minister, she now had to ensure that John Major would become her successor. She had learned to her horror that some of her friends were thinking of voting for Michael Heseltine. She did what she could to dissuade them.

Time for a new chapter

Margaret Thatcher spent her last weekend at the Prime Minister's official country residence, Chequers, arriving on the Saturday evening, having had lunch with family and friends at Number 10. She knew she would miss Chequers, and took the opportunity to walk round the rooms there one last time.

When the results of the second ballot came through, she was delighted. John Major had won 185 votes to Michael Heseltine's 131 and Douglas Hurd's 56. Major was two votes short of avoiding a third ballot, but both Hurd and Heseltine announced that they would support him. He was therefore deemed to be the new Prime Minister.

Mrs Thatcher's last day in office was Wednesday, 28 November. That morning, she left her flat and went to her study for the last time to check that nothing had been left behind, and was shocked to discover that she could not get in, because the key had already been removed from her key ring. As she said goodbye to the staff, she could not hold back her tears, hard as she tried.

And so we come to the point at which this book began, as Mrs Thatcher got into the car with Denis beside her, accompanied by the strobe effect of the photographers' flash guns. Margaret Thatcher was leaving Number 10 Downing Street for the last time as Prime Minister of Great Britain.

THE MUMMY REMAINS:

Margaret Battles On

❝ I shan't be pulling the levers, but I shall be a very good back-seat driver. ❞
1990

Is there life after premiership? There was – and continues to be – for Margaret Thatcher, or Baroness Thatcher, as she has now become. She continues to be a controversial figure, and, as she has never been backward in coming forward with her views on a variety of topics, she has often proved to be a thorn in the side of the succeeding administrations.

Her prime-ministerial days may have been over, but her days as an MP were not, and from the back benches Margaret Thatcher continued to make her views known, intervening in the Prime Minister's 28 March 1991 statement on the end of the Gulf War, speaking in a debate on Europe on 26 June, speaking in a debate on the Maastricht Treaty in November. At times, her determination to remain very much in the public eye made things very uncomfortable for her successor John Major.

On 7 December 1990, not long after bowing out tearfully from Number 10, she was awarded the Order of Merit by the Queen, and, five days later, she received the Freedom of the City of Westminster.

Not one to forget old friends, in February 1991 she gave the main speech at celebrations to mark the eightieth birthday of Ronald Reagan. After over thirty-three years in the House of Commons, Mrs Thatcher ceased to be an MP on the dissolution of Parliament on 16 March the following year for a general election, which the Tories won, in spite of wildly off-the-mark opinion polls that had everyone believing that Labour could break the Tory stranglehold on the country. On 30 June 1992, she was introduced into the House of Lords, making her maiden speech – on the subject of Europe – on 2 July.

A year later, Europe was again the subject of a controversial speech she made, specifically on the Maastricht Treaty.

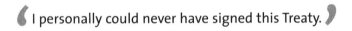

❛ I personally could never have signed this Treaty. ❜

In October 1996 – six months before a general election that would usher Labour back into power with a landslide victory – Baroness Thatcher called on Tories to unite behind John Major, and to 'get cracking' on a campaign to ensure Labour did not win. She appeared on the platform on the opening day of the Tory conference in Bournemouth, and later told activists in the party that it had never been more important for the Tories to be returned to government.

But it was Labour who were returned to power, albeit eighteen years after losing it, when they won a landslide victory, taking 419 seats to the Tories' 165 and the Liberal Democrats' 46, with other parties taking a further 29. Those who sat up into the early hours as result after result poured into newsrooms will remember how John Major – with what might have seemed to the public to be uncharacteristic humour – took the no doubt expected defeat with what appeared to be mock equanimity, when he told gathered party members, 'OK, we lost.'

> ❛ I do not accept the idea that all of a sudden Major is now his own man. There isn't any such thing as Majorism. ❜

At the Tory conference in October 1997, Baroness Thatcher criticized British Airways over its tail-fin design (it had dropped the Union flag in favour of something of a more international flavour). She famously visited the area where corporate stalls were set up, and fixed her eyes on a model of one of the offending aircraft, complete with offending tail fin, decorated with one of the offending design. Addressing her remarks to David Holmes, the BA corporate resources director, she said, 'We fly the British flag, not these awful things.' She said the design – from the Ncoakhoe tribe of the Kalahari – was 'terrible'. She delved into the famous handbag, produced a clean white handkerchief, draped it over said offending fin and ordered, 'Tape it up.' With Denis at her side, she swept out of the hall.

Blair: Thatcher's creature

Much has been said about just how much Tony Blair is Baroness Thatcher's creature. In December 1997, it was revealed that she had met Blair four times to brief him on foreign affairs (this was the first time she had returned to Number 10 since she had left it so tearfully back in November 1990). The Tory chairman, Brian Mawhinney, criticized Blair in 1996 for having likened himself in some ways to Mrs Thatcher. Many have commented, since the revelations over his consulting her, on how much he is influenced by her, and, of course, it has been said on many occasions that New Labour is merely Old Tory, that Blair and his cohorts have hijacked the old Labour Party and given it a blue rinse.

In addition to commenting on Britain's domestic and European policies, Baroness Thatcher has also found opportunities to involve herself on the world stage. In 1998, to the disgust of many in Britain and elsewhere, Baroness Thatcher found herself defending and supporting the former Chilean dictator, General Augusto Pinochet, who had been placed under house arrest while he was in the UK for medical treatment. There had been an extradition warrant for him to answer charges in Spain relating to human-rights abuses that had taken place during his rule. After much legal wrangling, the House of Lords upheld the extradition request, and Jack Straw, then the Home Secretary, allowed the procedure to continue. Eventually, Straw released Pinochet on humanitarian grounds, since he was allegedly ill.

An accolade to Baroness Thatcher's policies and ideals came from a source that would have been undreamed of some years before, when a new political party was launched in Russia, calling itself the Thatcherites of Russia. The audience at the party's launch were told by speaker after speaker that what Thatcher did for Britain, Thatcherism could do for Russia.

A handbag?

Margaret Thatcher's handbag was almost as famous as she was. Often it was said that someone had been 'handbagged', when Mrs Thatcher had had cause to offer words of criticism. Certainly it came to symbolize her style of leadership.

In July 2000 the famous and ubiquitous handbag – there were obviously several – received due recognition when a black leather number originally costing about $500 went for $150,000 (about £100,000) in an Internet auction in aid of a cancer charity. It was bought by a Scottish businessman.

Ten years after the fall

November 2000 saw the tenth anniversary of Mrs Thatcher's resignation as Prime Minister. There was criticism of her from beyond the grave, when a former Archbishop of Canterbury, Robert Runcie, left something of a time bomb in the form of a TV interview he had recorded a week before his death in July that year. Runcie, Archbishop from 1980 to 1991, had been criticized by the Thatcher government – and, predictably, by the tabloid press – for having prayed for the dead of both sides after the Falklands War.

In his posthumous broadcast, he confirmed that he had directed his remarks at the government of the time when he had attacked 'those who stay at home, most violent in their attitudes and untouched in themselves'. He told his interviewer for the programme, 'In the eighties there were huge events with which one could not fail to be associated ... For me there was a government that was successful in strengthening the economy and dealing with the unions and yet at the same time I could look out of the window at Lambeth Palace and see the fires of Brixton burning.

'There was a difficulty in recognizing firm government but [also] recognizing the damage done to the casualties of change and I had to speak up for them. I wasn't wholly convinced [Mrs Thatcher] was wrong, but I was convinced something had to be done about the effects of her policies that turned me into a wet, someone who was wobbly.'

More criticism came ten years after her fall from power from the current Prime Minister, Tony Blair, who savaged her in a repudiation of boom-and-bust economics. This was only months before the next general election, which Labour won in the spring of 2001.

Blair had tried to copy Mrs Thatcher's forceful

leadership style, and, as we have seen, there have been parallels drawn between the two leaders, but that was now being consigned to the history books. 'I take nothing away from those things that were done in the 1980s that we have kept,' he said during Prime Minister's Questions, 'but it really is time in my view that we move British politics beyond the time of Margaret Thatcher.'

We are in a new era. Today we have to deal with those problems that we inherited from that time – the boom-and-bust economics, the social division, the chronic under-investment in our public services. A sensible, modern attitude to Europe is what we need.

Baroness Thatcher had criticized Blair for his support of Britain's commitment of 12,500 troops to a European rapid-reaction force, which she had described as 'monumental folly', putting Britain's security at risk 'in order to satisfy political vanity'.

I prefer NATO and I prefer the great alliance between Britain, Europe and America ... it is that which was of great benefit to the world. We lost a lot of people on the Continent defending the liberty of our country and the countries of others, and we must never forget.

When that 2001 general election came, Labour were returned. But Baroness Thatcher had been on the campaign trail, dubbing her campaign 'the Mummy returns', after she had spotted a poster for a film of the same name.

In May 2001, Baroness Thatcher was quick to defend George W. Bush's plan to develop the so-called 'Son of Star Wars' – a global missile defence shield. She also urged Blair to support Bush and 'stop shilly-shallying'.

'The West is faced by an ever-increasing number of dangerous states with access to weapons of mass destruction,' she said in a statement. 'It is in all our interests that America should recognize and act speedily on this grave and growing threat.'

In August 2001, she was backing Iain Duncan Smith as the next leader of the party, to succeed William Hague. The alternative, Kenneth Clarke, a former Chancellor of the Exchequer, would, she said, steer the party to disaster.

After the attacks on the World Trade Center and the Pentagon on 11 September 2001, Baroness Thatcher criticized the response of Muslim leaders. She told *The Times*:

‘The people who brought down those towers were Muslims, and Muslims must stand up and say that that is not the way of Islam. Passengers on those planes were told that they were going to die, and there were children on board. They must say that it was disgraceful. I have not heard enough condemnation from Muslim priests.’

In January 2002, the nation heard that Margaret Thatcher had suffered a minor stroke, but was soon back in harness, as though nothing had happened. However, in March she announced the speaking was over – doctor's orders. There had, it was revealed, been a number of small strokes over recent months, not just one. The seventy-six-year-old baroness was about to embark on a busy speaking programme to promote her new book, *Statecraft*, but had had to cut back severely on her commitments.

In the spring of 2002, Baroness Thatcher paid tribute to the Queen Mother, who had died earlier that year. 'She was an inspiration during the dark days of war,' she said, 'and throughout her life she never failed to lift our spirits by her sense of duty. Her death is more than a source of grief to the royal family: it is an irreplaceable loss to the whole nation.'

Later that year – October – Baroness Thatcher had, it seemed, defied doctor's orders and was back on the platform again, speaking for more than five minutes at the opening of a foundation at Cambridge University that houses her political papers.

Baroness Thatcher was praising Tony Blair in December 2002 for backing the USA in its so-called 'war on terror'. She was speaking – still, one assumes, against doctor's orders – in Washington, DC, where she was honoured for her 'pursuit of political freedom'. She spoke to an audience of around eight hundred academics and senior politicians, calling Osama bin Laden and Saddam Hussein 'psychopaths'.

Off with her head!

Margaret Thatcher has managed to be rarely out of the headlines, even since her supposed retirement from public life. The latest development in the Thatcher story concerns a large marble statue of her. Baroness Thatcher had unveiled the statue in May 2001, saying it was bigger than she thought it would be, but that was only fitting for the country's first woman prime minister. Because of rules stating that a former prime minister had to have been dead for at least five years before his or her likeness can be exhibited in the Members' Lobby of the House of Commons, the eight-foot statue languished for several months in the studio of the man who sculpted it, Neil Simmons.

In the end the statue was exhibited in the Guildhall Art Gallery. In July 2002, however, in an attack which amply illustrates the powerful personal and political feelings Baroness Thatcher can still manage to evoke, Paul Kelleher, a theatre producer, attempted to decapitate the figure with a cricket bat before succeeding with an iron bar. After being arrested on charges of criminal damage, he was first brought to trial in December 2002. The jury could not decide whether he had a 'lawful excuse' for removing the Iron Lady's – or, in this case, the Marble Lady's – head. He defended the act as a protest against global capitalism, and as 'artistic expression and my right to interact with this broken world'. While he denied criminal damage as he was not a criminal, he did not deny having perpetrated the decapitation. When asked about his definition of criminal damage he responded: 'I can highlight all the criminal damage Margaret Thatcher caused by being in power.'

In a new trial in January 2003, thirty-seven-year-old Mr Kelleher was found guilty, and in February was jailed for three months for causing the lady to lose her head.

APPENDIX:

Margaret's Quotable Quotes

All quotations can be deemed to be from speeches, interviews or statements to the media unless a print source is given.

Before premiership

It will be years – and not in my time – before a woman will lead the party or become Prime Minister.
speech, 1974

I don't want to be leader of the party – I'm happy to be in the top dozen.
1974

I have changed everything.
1976

I must warn you, that, although our party is going to win overall, I could lose Finchley.
to her family on the eve of the general election, May 1979

If I lose, I will be out tomorrow.
on the day before 1979 general election

The better I do, the more is expected of me. I am ready for that. I think I have the strength to do anything that I feel has to be done.
September 1975

●

On becoming PM

Where there is discord, may we bring harmony. Where there is error, may we bring truth. Where there is doubt, may we bring faith. Where there is despair, may we bring hope.
quoting St Francis of Assisi on the steps of 10 Downing Street, May 1979

●

Party conference speeches

You will understand, I know, the humility I feel at following in the footsteps of great men like … Winston Churchill, a man called by destiny who raised the name of Britain to supreme heights in the history of the free world; in the footsteps of Anthony Eden, who set us the goal of a property-owning democracy – a goal we still pursue today; of Harold Macmillan, whose leadership

brought so many ambitions within the grasp of every citizen; of Alec Douglas-Home, whose career of selfless public service earned the affection and admiration of us all; and of Edward Heath, who successfully led the party to victory in 1970 and brilliantly led the nation into Europe in 1973. During my lifetime, all the leaders of the Conservative Party have served as prime minister. I hope the habit will continue.
first speech to conference as party leader, 1975

Let us be clear in our thinking. Let us be confident in our approach but, above all, let us be generous in our understanding.
leader's speech, 1976

I am very pleased with my promotion to Prime Minister. I much prefer this job to the other.
leader's speech, 1979

Through the long years of opposition you kept faith; and you will, I know, keep faith through the far longer years of Conservative government that are to come.
leader's speech, 1979

I believe the interests of Britain can now only be served by a third Conservative victory.
leader's party conference speech, closing remarks, 1986

There was, for instance, our election victory in June. They tell me that makes it three wins in a row. Just like Lord

Liverpool. And he was Prime Minister for fifteen years. It's rather encouraging.

leader's speech, 1987

We've laid the economic foundations of a decent and prosperous future. None of this would have been possible without the two finest Chancellors of the Exchequer since the war – Geoffrey Howe and Nigel Lawson.

leader's speech, 1989

The world needs Britain – and Britain needs us ...

leader's speech, 1989

●

The Opposition

Then I heard voices getting all worked up about someone they kept calling the 'Prime Minister-in-Waiting' [Neil Kinnock]. It occurs to me ... that he might have quite a wait. I can see him now, like the people queuing up for the winter sales. All got up with his camp bed, hot Thermos, woolly balaclava, CND badge ... Waiting, waiting, waiting ... And then, when the doors open, in he rushes – only to find that, as always, there's 'that woman' ahead of him again. I gather there may be an adjective between 'that' and 'woman', only no one will tell me what it is.

Thatcher on Kinnock, 1990

It's the Labour government that have brought us record peacetime taxation. They've got the usual socialist disease – they've run out of other people's money. And it's the Labour government that have pushed public spending to record levels. And how've they done it? By borrowing and borrowing and borrowing. Never in the field of human credit has so much been owed.
leader's speech, 1975

I sometimes think the Labour Party is like a pub where the mild is running out. If someone doesn't do something soon, all that's left will be bitter. And all that's bitter will be Left.
leader's speech, 1975

●

Edward Heath

We failed the people.
on the Heath government, Daily Telegraph, *February 1974*

As Ted Heath said with such force on Wednesday, Britain is at the end of the road, and as we all know, he is a man who never tells the truth to serve the hour. I am indeed grateful for what he said. Let us all have his courage.
leader's party conference speech, 1976

I've got my teeth into him and I'm not going to let go.
of Edward Heath, during leadership contest,
February 1975

Let me say at once that I am glad that Ted Heath addressed our conference and delighted that he will be helping us in the Croydon by-election.
leader's party conference speech, 1981

●

Socialism

It is no part of Conservative philosophy to help build a socialist Britain … the Conservative Party puts the national interest before shortterm party advantage … the Britain we are seeking is a Britain which could never be founded on socialism.
1976

Britain, beware! The signpost reads, 'This way to the total socialist state'.
1977

[L]et me tell you a little about my 'extremism'. I am extremely careful never to be extreme. I am extremely aware of the dangerous duplicity of socialism, and extremely determined to turn back the tide before it

destroys everything we hold dear. I am extremely disinclined to be deceived by the mask of moderation that Labour adopts whenever an election is in the offing … by all who would 'keep the red flag flying here'. Not if I can help it. The Conservative Party now and always flies the flag of one nation – and that flag is the Union Jack.
1977

The best reply to full-blooded socialism is not milk-and-water socialism, it is genuine conservatism.
1977

My job is to stop Britain going red.
The Times, *March 1977*

The country is looking for a sign that we can succeed where socialism has failed. Labour's dead end has to be our beginning.
1978

The Left continues to refer with relish to the death of capitalism. Well, if this is the death of capitalism, I must say that it is quite a way to go.
1980

Mr [Anthony] Wedgwood Benn says that 'the forces of socialism in Britain cannot be stopped'. They can be and they will be. We shall stop them. We shall stop them democratically, and I use the word in the dictionary sense, not the Bennite sense.
1981

We are only in our first term. But already we have done more to roll back the frontiers of socialism than any previous Conservative government.
1982

Our people will never keep the Red Flag flying here. There is only one banner that Britain flies, the one that has kept flying for centuries – the red, white and blue.
1983

A socialist party can only hope to survive in Britain by pretending that it is something else.
1983

In the Falklands we had to fight the enemy without. Here the enemy is within and it is much more difficult to fight, but just as dangerous to liberty.
referring to the miners in a speech to the 1922 Committee, July 1984

So it's back to square one for the socialists. The Labour leopard can't change its spots – even if it sometimes thinks wistfully of a blue rinse.
1988

[T]he trouble with Labour is that they're just not at home with freedom. Socialists don't like ordinary people choosing, for they might not choose socialism.
1989

And what a prize we have to fight for: no less than the chance to banish from our land the dark divisive clouds of Marxist socialism.
speech to Scottish Tories, 1983

●

Unemployment

Today our country has more than 2 million unemployed.
first year in office, 1980

The concern of this conference is focused on the plight of the unemployed. But we seek not only to display and demonstrate that concern but to find and pursue those policies which offer the best hope of more lasting jobs in future years.
1981

Now for the future, you heard from Norman Tebbit that every sixteen-year-old who leaves school next year will either have a job or a year of full-time training. Unemployment will not then be an option, and that is right.
1982

Our youth training scheme is the most imaginative in the Western world and when it is well under way every sixteen-year-old will have the choice either to stay on at school or to

find a job or to receive training. At that age, unemployment should not be an option. That is our objective.
1983

To have over 3 million people unemployed in this country is bad enough ... but to suggest, as some of our opponents have, that we do not care about it is as deeply wounding as it is utterly false.
fifth year in office, 1984

●

USSR

Soviet Marxism is ideologically, politically and morally bankrupt. But militarily the Soviet Union is a powerful and growing threat.
1980

The Soviet Union is unlikely to change much or quickly.
1983

I stand before you tonight in my green chiffon evening gown, my face softly made up, my fair hair gently waved. The Iron Lady of the Western world? Me? A Cold War warrior? Well, yes – if that is how they wish to interpret my defence of values and freedoms fundamental to our way of life.
speech, 1976, after being dubbed the Iron Lady

This weekend, President Reagan and Mr Gorbachev are meeting in Reykjavik. Does anyone imagine that Mr Gorbachev would be prepared to talk at all if the West had already disarmed? It is the strength and unity of the West which has brought the Russians to the negotiating table.
1986

This is a man I can do business with.
on first meeting Soviet President Mikhail Gorbachev

•

Europe

In Europe we have shown that it is possible to combine a vigorous defence of our own interests with a deep commitment to the idea and to the ideals of the Community.
1980

The British government intend to stand by both these great institutions, the Community and NATO. We will not betray them.
1980

At present, as you know, Britain pays quite large sums to Community partners often richer than we ourselves. That is fundamentally unjust. It is also short-sighted.
1982

No! No! No!
opposing proposals put forward by Jacques Delors, 1990

●

Cabinet colleagues

And to our present Chairman [Cecil Parkinson] may I say this: I want to let you into a secret. I asked Peter's [Thorneycroft, whom Mrs Thatcher had appointed as party chairman on her becoming leader] advice about you. With that characteristic caution and understatement he said, 'I think he'd do it rather well' – and so say all of us.
leader's party conference speech, 1981

We meet in the aftermath of a general election. I think we can say that the result was not exactly a photo finish. We are grateful for victory. We are grateful to you and the thousands of people in every part of the country who worked so hard to ensure success. We thank you all, and we do not forget today the man who so brilliantly organized the campaign [Cecil Parkinson].
leader's party conference speech, 1983

Mrs Thatcher categorized her ministers into those she could put down, those she could break down and those she could wear down.
Independent, *1993*

Every Prime Minister needs a Willie.
on William Whitelaw, 1991

The Chancellor is unassailable.
comment about Nigel Lawson only days before he resigned from the government, 1989

John Major, Peter Lilley and Michael Howard … Douglas Hurd and Tom King … Cecil Parkinson and John Gummer … David Waddington, Ken Clarke, Chris Patten, Tony Newton and John MacGregor, [and] Norman Lamont … What a fabulous team we've got.
leader's speech, 12 October 1990

They have hit at everything I believed in.
on John Major's government, 12 June 1995

I don't think I was unkind to him. I supported him a lot – I chose him!
referring to her successor, John Major, 23 June 1995

●

Privatization

I never thought that we should be able to make so much progress with denationalization in these first two and a half years. And I can assure you that there will be more of these measures in the next session of Parliament … [I]f this

is dogmatism then it is the dogmatism of Mr Marks and Mr Spencer, and I'll plead guilty to that any day of the week.
1981 (interestingly, Thatcher opts for the term 'denationalization', not 'privatization')

At national level, since the general election just over a year ago, the government has denationalized five major enterprises, making a total of thirteen since 1979 … Soon, we shall have the biggest ever act of denationalization with British Telecom, and British Airways will follow; and we have not finished yet.
1984

[M]illions have already become shareholders. And soon there will be opportunities for millions more, in British Gas, British Airways, British Airports and Rolls-Royce. Who says we've run out of steam? We're in our prime!
1986

We've trebled the number of shareholders in Britain and privatized twenty major industries. That's good, but not enough. We want more shareholders and more workers to own shares. So we'll privatize the major ports; then we'll tackle British Rail – with more to come.
1990

Doctor Johnson could have said: 'when you know you are going to be privatized, it concentrates the mind wonderfully.'
1986

Terrorism

Terrorism is a deadly threat to our way of life, and we will not be cowed by it. We will continue to resist it with all our power and to uphold the principles of democratic government.
1982

The terrorist threat to freedom is worldwide. It can never be met by appeasement. Give in to the terrorist and you breed more terrorism. At home and abroad our message is the same. We will not bargain, nor compromise, nor bend the knee to terrorists.
1988

The West is faced by an ever-increasing number of dangerous states with access to weapons of mass destruction.
2001

The U-turn

To those waiting with bated breath for that favourite media catchphrase, the 'U-turn', I have only one thing to say. 'You turn if you want to. The lady's not for turning.'
leader's party conference speech, 1980

Journalists, many but not all of them on the left, were almost daily predicting U-turns. Some indeed, confidently went around the bend.
leader's party conference speech, 1982

●

Greater London Council

[I]n the coming session of Parliament we shall introduce legislation which will abolish the GLC and the metropolitan county councils.
to conference, 1984

●

South Africa

Labour want sanctions against South Africa. Tens of thousands of people could lose their jobs in Britain – quite apart from the devastating consequences for black South Africans.
1986

If you want to cut your own throat, don't come to me for a bandage.
to Robert Mugabe, about imposing sanctions on South Africa

I am in step with the people of South Africa.
October 1989

●

Education

Comprehensive schools will have gone out in ten or fifteen years' time.
1970

Let our children grow tall, and some grow taller than others.
speech in the USA, 1975

●

Environment

The core of Tory philosophy and the case for protecting the environment are the same.
1988

Had we gone the way of France and got 60 per cent of our electricity from nuclear power, we should not have environmental problems.
speech, 1988

●

On herself

I wasn't lucky. I deserved it.
on receiving a school prize, aged nine

I am not hard – I'm frightfully soft. But I will not be hounded.
interview, 1972

If a woman like Eva Perón with no ideals can get that far, think how far I can go with all the ideals that I have.
interview, 1980

No one would have remembered the Good Samaritan if he'd only had good intentions. He had money as well.
television interview, 1980

I owe a great deal to the church for everything in which I believe. I am glad that I was brought up strictly ... I was a very serious child ... There was not a lot of fun and sparkle in my life.
Daily Telegraph, *June 1980*

Victorian values were the values when our country became great.
television interview, 1982

This is a day I was not meant to see.
on the day after the Brighton bomb, 1984

To wear your heart on your sleeve isn't a very good plan: you should wear it inside, where it functions best.
interview with Barbara Walters on ABC-TV, 18 March 1987

I think I have become a bit of an institution – you know the sort of thing people expect to see around the place.
speech, 1987

We have become a grandmother.
to reporters outside 10 Downing Street, 1989

The Mummy returns.
during the 2001 general election campaign, after passing a poster publicizing a film of that name

Feminism

What did it ever do for me?
on feminism

The battle for women's rights has been largely won.
1982

I don't like strident women.
date not known

I owe nothing to women's lib.
interview, 1982

●

Falklands

Failure? The possibilities don't exist.
on the Falklands War, 1982

It shows that the substance under test consists of ferrous metal of the highest quality. It is of exceptional tensile strength, resistant to wear and tear, and may be used with advantage for all national purposes.
Enoch Powell, on how Mrs Thatcher weathered the Falklands conflict

We knew what we had to do and we went about it and did it. Great Britain is great again.
on the end of the Falklands conflict

Rejoice! Just rejoice!
on the sinking of the Belgrano

●

NHS

The National Health Service is safe in our hands.
Conservative Party conference, 1983

She cannot see an institution without hitting it with her handbag.
Julian Critchley, Conservative MP and 'wet', 1982

●

1990 leadership contest

Having consulted widely among my colleagues, I have concluded that the unity of the party and the prospects of victory in a general election would be better served if I stood down to enable Cabinet colleagues to enter the ballot for the leadership.
statement, 22 November 1990

It's a funny old world.
comment after her decision to quit in November 1990, pointing out that she had never lost an election in her life, yet had been forced to stand down

Now where were we? I'm enjoying this.
an aside during a speech she made in the Commons only hours after announcing she would quit

I have never been defeated by the people. It is my great pride.
February 1991

Rejoice, rejoice!
attributed to Edward Heath, upon hearing the news of Mrs Thatcher's resignation

Thatcherism

We must have an ideology. The other side have got an ideology they can test their policies against. We must have one as well.
1975

I think, historically, the term 'Thatcherism' will be seen as a compliment.
speech, 1985

In Britain, we're all Thatcherites now.
at a party given in honour of her seventieth birthday, USA, 24 October 1995

I am told we are all Thatcherites now.
Daily Telegraph, *9 December 1996*

Thatcherism is not an ideology, but a political style: a trick of presenting reasonable, rather pedestrian ideas in a way that drives reasonable men into frothing rage.
Spectator, *1984*

A Short Bibliography

Campbell, John,
Margaret Thatcher – Volume 1: The Grocer's Daughter
(London: Pimlico, 2001).

Campbell, John,
Margaret Thatcher – Volume 2
(London: Pimlico, 2003).

Dale, Iain (ed.),
As I Said to Denis … The Margaret Thatcher Book of Quotations
(London: Robson Books, 1997).

Dale, Iain (ed.),
Memories of Maggie: A Portrait of Margaret Thatcher
(London: Politico's Publishing, 2000).

Daly, Macdonald, and George, Alexander,
Margaret Thatcher In Her Own Words
(London: Penguin, 1987).

Harris, Robin (ed.),
The Collected Speeches of Margaret Thatcher
(London: HarperCollins, 1997).

Thatcher, Margaret,
The Downing Street Years
(London: HarperCollins, 1993).

Thatcher, Margaret,
The Path to Power
(London: HarperCollins, 1995).

Thatcher, Margaret,
Statecraft
(London: HarperCollins, 2002).

●

World Wide Web sources

These websites give excellent information on the life and political philosophy of Margaret Thatcher, combining extracts from memoirs and speeches with chronologies and other interesting information.

www.margaretthatcher.com

www.margaretthatcher.org

www.thatcheronline.co.uk